A CAMPBELL JOURNEY

# A Campbell Journey

by
Ted A. Campbell

Tuckapaw Media
Dallas, Texas
2009

*A Campbell Journey*

by Ted A. Campbell
Copyright © 2009, Ted A. Campbell

Date of version: November 2, 2009

This work is licensed under the Creative Commons Attribu- tion-No Derivative Works 3.0 Unported License. To view a copy of this license, visit

> http://creativecommons.org/licenses/by-nd/3.0/

or send a letter to Creative Commons, 171 Second Street, Suite 300, San Francisco, California, 94105, USA.

The above referenced license provides that this distribution of *A Campbell Journey* may be copied freely so long as it is copied unaltered, with all copyright, title, and author statements intact.

The image of the Campbell boar's head crest used on the cover and the title page was produced by an artist who identified himself/herself only as "Celtus" and is licensed under the Creative Commons Attribution ShareAlike 3.0 License.

ISBN: 0-9820698-2-0
EAN-13: 978-0-9820698-2-0

Tuckapaw Media: http://www.tuckapaw.com

IN MEMORY OF

EVERETT ARDEN CAMPBELL
(1924-2002)

WHOSE LABORS IN OUR FAMILY GENEALOGY
LAID THE GROUNDWORK FOR THIS STUDY

*NE OBLIVISCARIS*

# Contents

List of Illustrations ............................................................ ix

Greeting from His Grace the Duke of Argyll ................ xi

Introduction ....................................................................... 1

Chapter 1: Scotland and the Ulster Scots ....................... 7

Chapter 2: Virginia ............................................................ 17

Chapter 3: Tennessee ........................................................ 41

Chapter 4: Texas ................................................................ 73

Conclusion ......................................................................... 89

Genealogical Information ................................................ 93

Historical Documents ...................................................... 111

Index ................................................................................... 121

## List of Illustrations

1. Scots Gaelic Psalter from the Synod of Argyle ...... 12
2. The Coast of Ireland from Kintyre, Scotland ......... 13
3. A Campbell Journey (map) ........................................ 16
4. The Old Stone Church, Timber Ridge, Virginia .... 19
5. Statesville, Wilson County, Tennessee ..................... 54
6. Thomas Campbell Home ............................................ 57
7. Readyville Mill built ca. 1870 .................................... 59
8. John Watson Campbell and Frances Tenpenny ..... 61
9. Portrait of James Allen Campbell ............................. 64
10. Jimmie, Lillie, and Johnny Campbell ..................... 75
11. Elam Allen Campbell ca. 1918.................................. 78
12. Elam and Verda Campbell ca. 1925......................... 80
13. Campbells at Readyville Mill 1970 ......................... 86

CHIEF

The Duke of Argyll
*MacCailein Mor*

HONORARY
CHIEF EXECUTIVE

Alastair Campbell of Airds
*Unicorn Pursuivant*

## Clan Campbell
INVERARAY CASTLE

INVERARAY
ARGYLL PA32 8XF
SCOTLAND

Oct 2009

Dear Mr. Campbell,

In today's world it is one of the great pastimes and incredibly satisfying to be able to sit down, pull together all the ancestral work that previous generations have hoarded away and present it in the form of a family history.

As I sat down and read 'A Campbell Journey', you cannot but admire the dedication and determination that our ancestors had. It makes you proud to know that we all came from the same Campbell family roots and that values which were important back in the 1700s are still relevant today. The Campbell family DNA project is doing a great job in linking us all together. My oldest son, born in 2004, was christened Archie in order to keep one of these family traditions going.

Many of the Campbells that made the trip to America came through Philadelphia and it is hoped that in 2010, under the direction of the St Andrew's Society of Philadelphia, a Monument to Scottish Immigration will be erected overlooking the Delaware river, on the banks where our ancestors would have disembarked on their journey to settle in America.

The Campbells played an important role and this book documents in great detail one branch of our great family.

Yours

Argyll

# INTRODUCTION

The motto of the Campbell family is *ne obliviscaris*, "do not forget," or in Scots dialect, "dinna' forget." This is a book of remembering, lest we forget those who went before us in the Campbell family. This is a story of a Campbell journey from Scotland to Virginia to Tennessee to Texas.

My own Campbell family came from Tennessee to Texas around 1907, a few years after oil was discovered (1901) at Spindletop near my home town of Beaumont, Texas. We returned occasionally to the ancestral home place of my grandfather in Cannon County, Tennessee.

Tracing the Campbell lineage beyond Cannon County, Tennessee, posed a considerable challenge. A Tennessee relative, Mr. Lloyd Campbell, reported to me two different family stories about the origins of our Campbell family in Tennessee. Both stories involved Archibald Campbell from Virginia. According to one version of the story, Archibald was from Botetourt County, Virginia. The other story had him originating in Bedford County, Virginia. Both of these counties are in the Appalachian mountains of western Virginia where there had been a large influx of settlers of Scottish ancestry, some directly from Scotland, others by way of Ulster in Northern Ireland ("Scots Irish" or "Ulster Scots").

I was particularly interested in Archibald Campbell who died in Cannon County, Tennessee, around

1871. He listed his age in the 1870 census as 108, which would have placed his birth around 1762. This was probably exaggerated—based on earlier census records, I would guess his birth was closer to 1770—but two other matters interested me about him. First, the name "Archibald" was a very traditional name for the Campbell family (clan) in Argyll, Scotland. It is a typical name of the earls and later dukes of Argyll who serve as the head of clan Campbell. Second, although he may have exaggerated his age in his later years, Archibald Campbell consistently stated that he was born in Virginia. I knew that he would be our link to the deeper Campbell past.

In 2006-2007 I found very strong evidence tying our Campbell family and specifically Archibald Campbell to forebears in Wilson County, Tennessee, which lies to the northwest of Cannon County. Since then I have been working with materials about the Campbells in Wilson County and their Virginia origins. This has made clear the connection with Botetourt County, Virginia, that Lloyd Campbell had related to me, and it has also led to the knowledge of our Campbell immigrant ancestor, Malcolm Campbell.

The narrative given in this book covers roughly 250 years from about 1748 through the beginning of the twenty-first century. It is a story of a family journey in four stages: from Scotland (probably by way of Northern Ireland) to Virginia (Augusta County and Botetourt County) then to Tennessee (Wilson County and Cannon County) and from there to Texas (Jefferson County).

The chapters in this book follow these four stages of our Campbell family journey.

I have information on many branches of our family tree, but this book focuses on a particular narrative from father to son all bearing and bequeathing the surname Campbell through seven successive generations. Briefly stated, this succession of fathers and sons is as follows:

Malcolm Campbell
born about 1715 in Scotland or Northern Ireland

William Campbell
born about 1750 in colonial Virginia

Archibald Campbell
born about 1770 in colonial Virginia

Thomas Campbell
born in 1807 in Tennessee

John Watson Campbell
born in 1845 in Tennessee

James Allen Campbell
born in 1872 in Tennessee

Elam Allen Campbell
born in 1898 in Tennessee

This book also traces out four generations of the Campbell journey beyond Elam Campbell. Much more genealogical and family information on each of these will be given in what follows.

One of the matters that has concerned me in writing this book has to do with the fact that one ancestor, William Campbell of Botetourt County, Virginia, owned slaves and named these slaves in his will (see Item 3 in the Historical Documents section at the end of the book). Thinking about this, I recalled that I had first become interested in genealogy in the fall of 1976 at the time when Alex Haley's *Roots* was televised in the US, and I remember the blue-haired DAR ladies at the Clayton Genealogical Library in Houston trying to assist young black people interested in finding out about their own family histories. I have been careful, then, to name the names of slaves as members of a larger household that was our family in the hope that naming them may make it possible for future historians and genealogists to trace the journey of their families.

Historical scholarship is always tentative, and the following narrative represents the best knowledge that we have to date on this family and its history. Such recently available tools as internet-accessible genealogical databases and DNA testing have enabled this research and in the future new developments will almost certainly add new knowledge and insights and may even challenge some of the information contained in this account. Let the reader be warned about how historians write. There is a big difference between writing "Family information handed down by the Campbells of Roanoke states that Malcolm Campbell came to Virginia from Philadelphia," and writing "Malcolm Campbell came to Virginia from Philadelphia."

I am grateful to many persons who have helped in the making of this book. Mr. Lloyd Campbell of Woodbury, Tennessee, has consistently helped our family in connecting our stories to those of the Campbells in Tennessee, and we are all in his debt. I want to express my deep gratitude to His Grace the Duke of Argyll, the head of clan Campbell, who has graciously provided a greeting for the book. My father, Gene Allen Campbell, has read the manuscript and made many notes from which I have derived material for the book.

This book is dedicated to the memory of my uncle Everett Arden Campbell (1924-2002), my father's older brother. Everett was an ardent practitioner of both genealogy and photography. He encouraged my interests in both of these areas and this book carries forward both of these interests. I have utilized much of Everett's genealogical information in the book and some of the photographs that appear here are my scans of his own photographs of photos that had been handed down in the Campbell family. I wish Uncle Everett could see this book.

Ted A. Campbell
Commemoration of the Faithful Departed
November 2, 2009

## CHAPTER 1
## SCOTLAND AND THE ULSTER SCOTS

The Campbells are one of the primary families of Scotland and our Campbell forefathers through all the generations we know have taken the surname of this Scottish family or clan.

**Campbell DNA**

DNA testing confirms a very general connection between our male ancestors and the Campbell family. The field of genetic genealogy is still in its infancy, but DNA testing is able to identify general ethnic groups and subgroups, technically referred to as haplogroups, with increasing accuracy. In the summer of 2009 I submitted cheek-swab samples for testing through the Campbell Surname Project sponsored by familytreedna.com. The test results revealed only one Campbell relative with whom I am an exact match, and this match was at the level of 12 genetic markers, so it might be a very distant match. The other Campbell man was not tested at higher (25- or 37-marker) levels, so we do not know if we are a perfect match at those levels. But the testing did show that the DNA of my Y chromosomes, the DNA inherited by sons from their fathers in a direct patrilineal sequence, is of a haplogroup that is currently designated R1b1b2.

Test results to date in the Campbell Surname Project sponsored by familytreedna.com show that 90% of men tested who have the surname Campbell belong to haplogroup R1b1b2.[1] This does not mean that R1b1b2 is simply the Campbell family: it is a larger group that includes most of the men who carry the surname Campbell. What it means for our family is that our Campbell men are from the same genetic stock as most other Campbells who are descendants of the historic Campbell family of Scotland.

The DNA testing did reveal one interesting aspect of our deeper family history and that is a genetic connection to a family with the surname Ballew or some variant of it. The test results showed a perfect match at the 12-marker level with three men whose surnames are Ballew, Balliew, and Bilyeu. At a level of 25 DNA markers, two of these folks (Ballew and Balliew) were a match at 23 of 25 markers. This slightly imperfect match means that our male lines probably diverged between about 10-16 generations ago, and that probably (but not certainly) means that they diverged before our ancestors came to America, nine generations before me.[2]

Genetic genealogy is revealing that neither bloodlines nor surnames are as consistent as we might have thought in the past. Families are complicated affairs. Rather than saying we are perfect Y-chromosome

---

[1] Reported on the web page for the Campbell Surname Project sponsored by familytreedna.com:

http://www.familytreedna.com/public/Campbell/

[2] A Ballew family DNA project shows a division of men with variants of the surname Ballew into two major genetic groups, one of which is descended from haplogroup I2b1, and the other of which is descended from haplogroup R1b1b2 (the same as the majority of Campbell men): http://www.ballewassn.org/dna_project.htm.

descendants of the Scottish Campbells, it is more accurate to say that our forefathers are of the same genetic group as the Campbell family of Scotland and through all the generations we know, our male ancestors have identified themselves with the name of the Campbell family of Scotland.

## The Campbell Family in Scottish History

The connection between our family and the Campbells of Scotland should be obvious not only from the surname but also from certain personal names that appeared among eighteenth-century Campbells of our lineage: Malcolm and Archibald are typical Scots names, and Archibald in particular was a name long associated with the earls and dukes of Argyll who traditionally serve as the head or chief of clan Campbell. Other family names such as John, William, James, Edward, and Amos, were common to English as well as Scots, but were names frequently used in Scots families.

A recent historical study, *The Campbells: 1250-1513* by Stephen Boardman (2006), gives a detailed chronicle of the rise of the Campbell family to prominence in late medieval Scotland.[3] Boardman points out that there are mythical genealogies of the early Campbell leaders, some of which trace their ancestry to the legendary British King Arthur. These are historically useless but documentable historical figures who bear the Campbell name appear from the early thirteenth

---

[3] Stephen Boardman, *The Campbells: 1250-1513* (Edinburgh: John Donald, 2006).

century (the 1200s AD).[4] One of the early Campbell leaders was Colin Campbell (d. ca. AD 1296) known as "Colin the Great" whose descendants, including the later earls and dukes of Argyll, took the title *Mac Cailein Mór*, the son (or descendant) of Colin the Great.[5] These early Campbell leaders became allied with the Stewart family in the area around the Firth of Clyde in the southwest of Scotland. They became staunch supporters of Robert I, King of Scots, known commonly as Robert the Bruce, who reigned from 1306 to the time of his death in 1329.[6]

By the end of the fifteenth century the landowners of the Campbell family had gathered feudal contracts and titles that eventuated in the naming of another Colin Campbell who died in 1492 or 1493 as the first Earl of Argyll. Boardman argues against a conventional depiction of the Campbell leaders as lowland collaborators with the English throne. Rather, he depicts them as crafty political and military leaders who maintained the Celtic culture of Scotland.[7] The Campbells were never reigning monarchs but they served in the highest advisory positions to the reigning monarchs and they accumulated massive property (and the proceeds from that property) in Argyll and elsewhere in the west of Scotland.

---

[4] Ibid., pp. 9-27.

[5] The title appears on the letterhead of the Duke of Argyll in this book.

[6] Ibid., pp. 36-49.

[7] Ibid., passim.

In the seventeenth century the Campbell earls of Argyll supported Protestantism and specifically the form of religiously tolerant Protestantism that prevailed under William of Orange and his consort Mary who held the British throne from 1688 through 1702. Two Campbell earls had been beheaded prior to the reign of William and Mary for the suspicion that they did not support the Catholic-leaning kings Charles II and James II. Under William and Mary, the Campbell earl was granted the title Duke of Argyll, which continues to this day (see the greeting from the current Duke).

The leaders of clan Campbell, then, wielded considerable power in late medieval Scotland. But the Campbell clan or family in Scotland was a very large extended family, most of whose members did not own property and served as farmers or herders or worked in the fishing industry. Farmers and herders rented the lands they used from the landholders or lords (in Scots dialect "lairds") of the clan. They traditionally looked to the head of the clan for protection and in return pledged their support for the clan leader and their kindred.

Until the eighteenth century most Campbell people spoke the Scots Gaelic language, a Celtic language not to be confused with the "Scots" language that sounds like a dialect of English. From the time of the Reformation they adhered to the Church or "Kirk" of Scotland which had been reformed along the lines suggested by John Calvin in Geneva. Calvinistic reforms were put in place in Scotland by John Knox and other Scottish Reformers. The resulting church maintained a presbyterian form of church government, and when congregations and presbyteries of the Church of Scotland were organized in North America they were called Presbyterian churches.

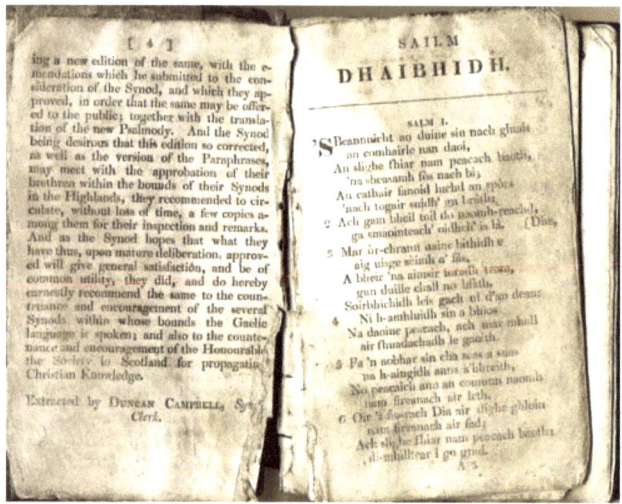

Scots Gaelic Psalter
authorized by the Synod of Argyle (Argyll) in 1783;
clerk of the synod was Duncan Campbell

**Scots, Ulster Scots, and America**

In the middle ages, the prosperity of the clan as a whole depended on the success of its landholders and leaders. But traditional relationships such as the clan began to break apart at the end of the middle ages and thereafter. Life became especially difficult for traditional Scottish farmers and herders in the 1600s and 1700s. For one thing, rents on agricultural lands were raised. A series of droughts, moreover, had disastrous consequences for agriculture. From the early 1700s landowners intent on agricultural reforms "cleared" farmers and herders from the lands they had traditionally leased in both lowland and highland Scotland. Laws were changed in such a way that tenants could no longer appeal to their clan chieftains for protection. The result was that Scottish farmers and herders began to seek other places to carry on agricultural life.

One option for them that opened up in the early years of the 1600s was a colony in the northernmost province of Ireland called Ulster, consisting of nine counties in which traditional land rights were abrogated by King James VI of Scotland who had become James I of England.

The coast of Ulster (Ireland, in the distance)
seen from the Mull of Kintyre (Scotland)

It was not a difficult passage from Scotland to Ireland. Scotland and Ireland had been closely related throughout their earlier histories with frequent migrations of peoples back and forth in the middle ages. In fact, it is not a great distance at all from the Campbell country of Scotland to Ulster. From the tip of the Kintyre Peninsula, the Mull of Kintyre, one can see the coast of northern Ireland across a twelve-mile strait, easily and often crossed since prehistoric times.

King James encouraged Scottish farmers to claim lands in Ulster and he also encouraged Scots Presbyterian clergy to settle in Ulster, developing congregations among the "Ulster Scots" population there. From 1625 a series of religious revivals occurred among the Ulster Scots Presbyterians, giving their religious tradition a distinctly evangelical or revivalistic character.[8]

From the early 1700s many Scots were attracted to settlement in North America. Some came directly from Scotland and some came from Ulster. It has been estimated that between 1718 and 1775 at least 150,000 Ulster Scots emigrated from northern Ireland to the American colonies that became the United States.[9] In America, the Ulster Scots settlers came to be known as "Scotch Irish" or "Scots Irish." Most of them identified themselves as Presbyterians, and their form of Presbyterianism tended to be evangelical and revivalistic in contrast to the staid, traditional Presbyterianism of the East Coast of the British North American colonies.

Ulster Scots settlers in the 1700s tended to arrive in North America through the port of Philadelphia but they found that the East Coast was already populated by earlier waves of immigrants. They turned inland to frontier areas to find farmland and that meant the Appalachian Mountains and their foothills. Some of them

---

[8] Marilyn Westerkamp, *The Triumph of the Laity* (New York: Oxford University Press, 1988), pp. 15-42 on the origins of the revival in 1625, pp. 141-164 on the transportation of the revival among Ulster Scots (and other Presbyterians) in colonial North America.

[9] David Hackett Fischer, *Albion's Seed: Four British Folkways in America* (New York: Oxford University Press, 1989), pp. 608-609 (including footnote 7 on p. 608).

proceeded directly west to Chester County or Lancaster County, Pennsylvania. But Scots Irish settlers very soon began bypassing these places and turned south at Gettysburg to enter the great Shenandoah Valley of Virginia. It was among these Scottish Presbyterian settlers to the Shenandoah Valley frontier that our Campbell ancestors appeared.

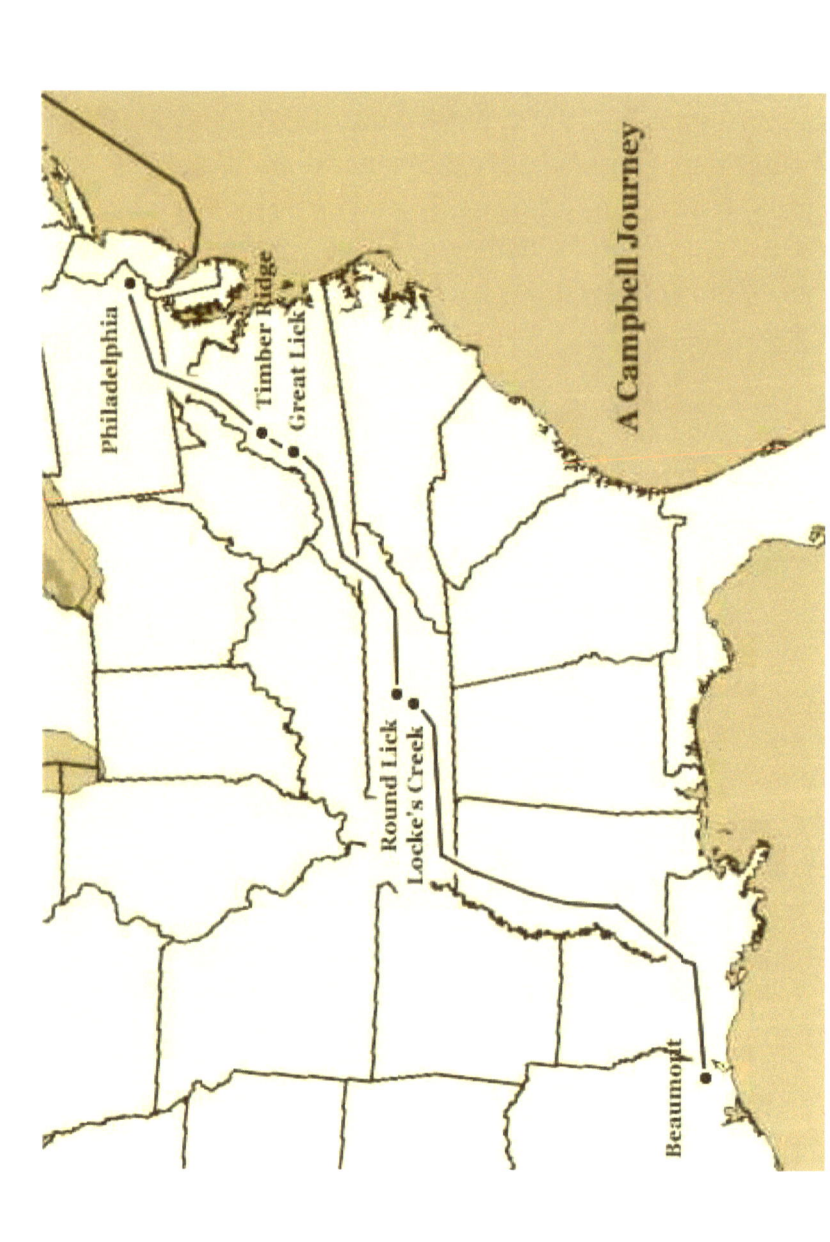

## Chapter 2
## Virginia

The Shenandoah Valley of Virginia runs roughly from north-northeast to south-southwest for more than 300 miles beginning in Pennsylvania at its northern extent and ending in the Holston River region of Tennessee at its southern extent. It is bounded by the Blue Ridge on its eastern side and by the greater mass of the Appalachians on the west. The long trail through the Valley, an old Indian trail, came to be known as "the Great Road" and it was a conduit for settlement that differed from the typical east-to-west pattern of frontier settlement in British North America and the US. Settlement in the Valley typically proceeded from north to south although settlers might take trails like the Western Road towards Kentucky or Tennessee from the lower reaches of the Valley.

Thousands of Ulster Scots settled in the Shenandoah Valley from the early eighteenth century.[10] Four early settlements of Ulster Scots settlers in the Shenandoah Valley were located within the early bounds of Augusta County and these formed a sequence along the Valley from north to south following the general direction of settlement:

---

[10] Fischer details the migrations of Scots and Scots-Irish peoples to North America in the period between 1717 and 1775 as the fourth group of American settlers he considers, pointing to western Virginia as one of the strongholds of Scots and Scots-Irish settlement.

a. Beverley Manor, founded in 1736, the site of present-day Staunton, Virginia, which remains the county seat of Augusta County

b. the Borden Tract, founded in 1737, immediately south of and adjoining Beverley Manor

c. Timber Ridge, settled around 1741, and now in Rockbridge County, about 32 miles south of Staunton

d. the Great Lick or Big Lick, settled around 1748, which later became the city of Roanoke and is now in Roanoke County, about 88 miles south of Staunton

The Timber Ridge community is of particular interest to our narrative because our immigrant ancestor seems to have been familiar with it. Among its early settlers was Archibald Alexander who along with his wife Margaret (Parks) Alexander had migrated to Pennsylvania from Ulster and had first settled in New Providence, Lancaster County, Pennsylvania. Alexander had moved into the Timber Ridge community by 1746 and would become one of its most prominent citizens as well as one of the justices of Augusta County.[11] His grandson, who bore the same name, was a Presbyterian clergyman and the first Principal of Princeton Theological Seminary. Another early settler was Daniel Lyle, who migrated from Ireland to Virginia and settled at Timber Ridge in 1745. He also became a prominent

---

[11] Oren F. Morton, *History of Rockbridge County, Virginia* (Staunton, Virginia: McClure Company, 1920), p. 244.

member of the community. The Rev. John Blair, a minister of the Presbytery of Donegal in Lancaster County, Pennsylvania, organized a Presbyterian congregation at Timber Ridge around 1746, and ten years later members of the congregation including Archibald Alexander and Daniel Lyle completed building the "Old Stone Church" which remains to this day as an active congregation of the Presbyterian Church in the USA. At about the same time as the building was constructed, a vigorous religious revival took place in the Timber Ridge community spurred on by fervent Presbyterian preaching.

The Old Stone Church built in 1756 at Timber Ridge, Virginia

A few feet from the Old Stone Church is a group of historical markers identifying the site where Sam Houston was born on March 2, 1793. Houston was from a prominent Scots-Irish Presbyterian family that had settled in the Timber Ridge community. His westward trek would take him to Wilson County, Tennessee, where our Campbell forebears would later settle, and thence to Texas where he became the first President of the Republic of Texas and then the first Governor of the State of Texas.

Our Virginia story begins with Malcolm Campbell, a settler connected to the Timber Ridge community and possibly to the Houston family there who appears in historical records as one of the first settlers further south on the Great Lick from 1748.

### Malcolm and Isabella (Huston) Campbell

We do not know precisely when or where Malcolm Campbell was born or when he came to Virginia but some information about him has been handed down by Campbell descendants still in the area of Roanoke, Virginia, where Malcolm settled. The information handed down among the Roanoke Campbells states that Malcolm:

> Came to Big Lick when boys were grown, from Pennsylvania. Landed in Philadelphia from Ireland. Was in area in 1740s. Had land grant in Roanoke of 440 acres and a house at Lick Spring where the Bridge and Ironworks are now. Furnished the French and Indian war with supplies in 1758.[12]

The expression "where the Bridge and Ironworks are now" is a local reference, that is, intended for hearers or readers familiar with Roanoke.

Family stories cannot always be trusted but in favor of this account is the fact that it coheres with the general pattern of settlement by Ulster Scots in colonial North America in a period of intense migration that occurred between 1718 and 1775. This wave of settlement

---

[12] From Stephen A. Taylor, who is himself a ninth-generation descendant of Malcolm currently living in Roanoke. Stephen had this information from William Wayne Campbell (b. 1926), a seventh-generation descendant of Malcolm who grew up in Roanoke, and William Wayne Campbell indicated that he had the information from Frank Pleas Campbell (1881-1955), a fifth-generation descendant of Malcolm Campbell.

is described in David Hackett Fischer's *Albion's Seed: Four British Folkways in America* (1989).[13] Fischer's work explains that the largest group of immigrants in this period were Ulster Scots migrating from Northern Ireland and their most frequently used port of entry was Philadelphia.[14] Fischer explains that the new immigrants "moved rapidly westward from Philadelphia into the rolling hills of the interior" and "gradually became the dominant English-speaking culture in a broad belt of territory that extended from the highlands of Appalachia through much of the old Southwest" including the Shenandoah Valley.[15] The family narrative about Malcolm coheres with this general historical narrative and the date given for his provisioning for the French and Indian War (1758) coheres with the general period of that conflict (1754-1763). Family information passed down from the Roanoke Campbells also states that Malcolm's father's name was Archibald Campbell and that his wife was Isabella Huston.[16]

---

[13] This wave of settlement of Irish, Scottish, and northern English immigrants to colonial North America is described in Fischer, pp. 605-639.

[14] Ibid., pp. 608-609 (including footnote 7 on p. 608, on the numbers of Ulster Scots) and p. 633 (on Philadelphia as a favored port of entry).

[15] Ibid., pp. 633-634 (quotations) and more generally pp. 633-639.

[16] An extended account on an internet discussion from 2004 is as follows: "Archibald Campbell, b. on Island of Jura, off the coast of Argyll, Scotland. He came to the American Colonies about 1740, along with sons; Malcolm, James, John and William Campbell. Malcolm b. 1720 in Argyllshire, Scotland, d. June 1763 at Big Lick, VA. James emigrated to Bladen Co., NC. He acquired a 600 acre land grant there. We think John settled in N.Y. with the info we have. William, we haven't any additional information on him at present. Malcolm Campbell came to Big Lick when his children were grown from PA." I cannot ascertain the source of this information.

Many genealogical reports, in contrast to the family traditions given above, claim that Malcolm came directly from Scotland and specifically from the island of Jura which lies off the coast of Argyll. These reports sometimes cite a passenger list for 1740 that included a Malcolm Campbell from the island of Islay (not Jura), but the printed version of this passenger list indicates that this Malcolm Campbell from Islay settled in New York.[17] Campbell family genealogy researchers may be predisposed to claim a direct Scottish connection, but the account handed down in the Roanoke Campbell family about Malcolm's coming from Northern Ireland rings true with historical circumstances.

Malcolm Campbell's date of birth can be only roughly estimated from other facts. His oldest child was born in 1743 and that means he was likely to have been born before 1723 although any time between 1700 and 1725 is possible. I would estimate that he was born between 1710 and 1717.

A problem with the account cited above from the Roanoke Campbell descendants is its claim that Malcolm Campbell "Came to Big Lick when boys were grown, from Pennsylvania." This could not be correct with reference to Malcolm's own children who were born from the 1740s, the very decade in which Malcolm appeared at the Great Lick. Moreover, Malcolm's children included girls as well as boys. Another version of

---

[17] David Dobson, *Directory of Scottish Settlers in North America, 1625-1825* (multiple volumes; Genealogical Publishing Company), 2:27. Dobson indicates that this Malcolm Campbell "settled in New York State."

the immigrant story maintains that it was Malcolm's father Archibald Campbell who came to Pennsylvania with his own boys including sons James, John, and William Campbell as well as Malcolm.[18] Perhaps "Came to Big Lick when boys were grown" refers to the coming of Malcolm and his own brothers from Pennsylvania to Virginia rather than the coming of Malcolm's children, although I cannot verify the source of this version of the story.[19]

Malcolm Campbell appeared first in historical records from 1748-1750 describing the Great Lick (later Roanoke) area but there is evidence that he had been connected to the the Timber Ridge community that had been settled before Great Lick. Malcolm's 1761 will names as witnesses Archibald Alexander and Daniel Lyle mentioned above as early and prominent settlers in the Timber Ridge community.[20] This connection to Timber Ridge suggests that he had been in that community and perhaps had settled there for some period prior to moving on south to the Great Lick.

Malcolm Campbell married a woman named Isabella Huston (or "Houston") who is named as his former wife in his 1761 will. Huston was a prominent

---

[18] See the extended account of the settlement of Archibald Campbell and sons Malcolm, William, James, and John Campbell in the footnote above.

[19] This account seems connected to the account given by the Roanoke Campbells because it continues with the line "Malcolm Campbell came to Big Lick when his children were grown from PA" which also appears in the account from the Roanoke Campbells.

[20] Will of Malcolm Campbell, dated 23 February 1761; Augusta County, Virginia, Will Book 3, page 266; cf. Kegley, *Virginia Frontier*, p. 182.

Ulster Scots surname and it is tempting to suggest that she was part of the Houston family of Timber Ridge that included the forebears of Sam Houston. Sam Houston himself left an extensive report of his family including references to a number of Houston women named Isabella, but I cannot identify any particular one of them who could have been the Isabella who married Malcolm Campbell.[21]

By March 1750 Malcolm and Isabella Campbell were living at the Big Lick or Great Lick, then in Augusta County, Virginia. An account of Malcolm living in this area is given in F. B. Kegley's *Virginia Frontier* (1938):

> Thomas Walker found Malcolm Campbell at the Great Lick in March 1750, and bought corn from him. How long he had lived there we do not know. In that same year he was a purchaser at Charles Hungate's sale. The only land associated with his name was a survey for forty-two acres on Evans' Spring Branch made in April 1751. On this land he probably lived until he purchased from John Smith the tract of 400 acres including the Great Lick. Edward McDonald had an account with him for currying and tanning leather from 1748.[22]

One problem with this account is that Dr. Thomas Walker's journal, on which Kegley's account is based,

---

[21] A letter from Sam Houston dated 3 May 1820; cited in S. R. Houston, *Brief Biographical Sketches of Some Descendants of the Houston Family* (1888), pp. 7-8.

[22] F. B. Kegley, *Kegley's Virginia Frontier: The Beginning of the Southwest, the Roanoke of Colonial Days, 1740-1783* (Roanoke, Virginia, 1938), p. 333.

actually states that it was from a Michael Campbell rather than Malcolm Campbell that Walker purchased corn for his horses at Great Lick. Kegley or some other subsequent interpreter may have presumed that this was actually Malcolm given the further information that Malcolm had established an account with Edward McDonald in that area from 1748 and had bought property nearby in 1751.

Malcolm and Isabella had children born from the 1740s: Archibald (1743), Elizabeth (1747), Mary (1749), William (ca. 1750), Rebecca (1751), and Jane (1754), who is apparently referred to as "Jean" in Malcolm Campbell's will. To avoid confusion with subsequent generations in what follows, I will refer to his sons Archibald and William as "Archibald Campbell the elder" and "William Campbell the elder." Malcolm's oldest daughter Elizabeth Campbell married William Simpson and their family would become tied up with the Campbells in the account of migrations following.

**Family of Malcolm Campbell (ca. 1750 - 1804)**

m. Isabella Huston (Houston)

Archibald Campbell    b. 1743

Elizabeth Campbell    b. 1747

Mary Campbell    b. 1749

William Campbell    b. ca. 1750

Rebecca Campbell    b. 1751

Jane (Jean) Campbell    b. 1754

Public documents give some hints of the life of Malcolm and Isabella Campbell on the colonial Virginia frontier. Kegley states that "In 1751 [Malcolm Campbell] was a juror who 'stayed' a case in court by jumping out of the Courthouse window and talking with other persons."[23] In the same year he purchased 42 acres of land on Evans Spring Branch.[24] In 1753 he was listed among workers on a road built from William Carvin's plantation to William Bryan's.[25] Two years later he was named as a constable in Augusta County.[26]

The account of Malcolm Campbell given by family members from Roanoke (above) mentions his provisioning British forces during the French and Indian War in 1758. One of the causes of that war (1754-1763) was the claim that France made to territories west of Virginia. Although most of the battles of the French and Indian War were fought in New York, Pennsylvania, and Canada, the Battle of Great Cacapon on April 18, 1756, was fought in Hampshire County, Virginia. This area, now part of the state of West Virginia, was a county of colonial Virginia adjacent to Augusta County in Malcolm Campbell's time.

---

[23] Ibid., p. 333.

[24] Ibid., p. 100.

[25] Ibid., p. 103.

[26] Ibid., p. 106 and cf. p. 183; at this point Kegley refers to Lyman Chalkley, *Chronicles of the Scotch-Irish Settlement in Virginia: Extracted from the Original Court Records of Augusta County, 1745-1800* (3 vols.; Rosslyn, VA: Commonwealth Printing Co., 1912), 2:419.

Within a few years of that battle, the war affected Malcolm Campbell's family directly. In 1760 a Williamsburg, Virginia, newspaper reported:

> Houses of Malcolm Campbell, J. Mason, J. Neely, and J. Bane, on Roanoke in Augusta, attacked by about 80 Cherokees. Indians beaten off. Major Lewis and Capt. Gist on the scout. Consternation of inhab's. Major Buchanan and others have removed—signs of enemy as far down as Loney's Ferry.[27]

This was likely an incident connected with the on-going war. American Indians were allied with the French, and the newspaper report notes that British officers led the pursuit against them.

It was during the period of the French and Indian War that Malcolm Campbell made a very large purchase of land. On November 21, 1759, he purchased from John Smith "400 acres on Goose Creek of Roanoke, including the Great Lick on west side of Smith's Creek near mouth of Lick Branch."[28] This was the property that was to become the City of Roanoke, Virginia, and for this reason Malcolm Campbell is considered to be one of the pioneering settlers of the Roanoke area. One of the central streets of the City of Roanoke, Campbell Avenue, is named for him.

Malcolm Campbell thus became an important landholder in Augusta County and he tried to live a life commensurate with that status although as we will see

---

[27] Cited in the *Virginia Magazine of History and Biography* (1908), p. 207.

[28] In Kegley, *Virginia Frontier*, p. 110. A facsimile of this indenture from John Smith to Malcolm Campbell is given on p. 108.

he ended up bequeathing considerable debts to his children. An enumeration of his estate reveals further details about the life he lived. The estate included "wagons and gears, farm tools, bells, wool-cards, blankets, chest, wagon-cloth, serge cloth, large jacket and great-coat. There were more than thirty horses, colts, fillies, etc., chiefly blacks and bays."[29] No slaves were mentioned in his will although his sons Archibald and William (below) would own slaves. Some of Malcolm's debts were paid off after his death with large amounts of whiskey (11 gallons), rum (15 gallons), and tobacco (290 pounds) that remained in his estate. This also reveals something about the daily culture of Malcolm Campbell's family. When his son William divorced his first wife Elizabeth (see the account following), he accused her of excessive drinking. She may have acquired that taste from the Campbells. Many of the expenses he owed were to various individuals who had assisted him in catching horses.[30]

The 1761 will of Malcolm Campbell refers to his "Ex.-Wife Isabella," indicating that he had separated from her at some point prior to 1761 but, one assumes, after 1754 when their last child was born. We do not have any indication why this separation came about.

Malcolm Campbell made out his will in 1761 and died in 1763 (see the summary of his will in the Historical Documents section below, Item 1). Although it named his former wife Isabella as executrix, she refused

---

[29] Kegley, *Virginia Frontier*, p. 333.

[30] Kegley, *Virginia Frontier*, pp. 333-334; this refers to Augusta County Will Book 4, p. 166.

to serve in this role, which denotes that she was an intelligent woman. Malcolm's daughter Elizabeth (Campbell) Simpson petitioned the court and was named as Malcolm's executrix. She and her husband William Simpson struggled to pay off weighty debts that were owed after the death of Malcolm. The total amount of proceeds from the sale of Malcolm's property came to £ 133/4/1 (these amounts refer to pounds sterling, shillings, and pence). The total amount of debts came to £ 219/9/11,[31] leaving the sum of £ 86 owed by the executors. According to one accounted (undocumented), William Simpson spent two months in jail as a result of these debts.

## William and Elizabeth (McDonald?) and Susannah (Dabney) Campbell

Malcolm Campbell's son William Campbell (the elder) inherited 200 acres of Malcolm's property on Great Lick including the homestead. He married a woman named Elizabeth whose surname does not appear in public documents. Family tradition passed on among the Campbells of Roanoke held that her name was Rebecca McDonald, but the personal name Rebecca is inconsistent with court records that name her as Elizabeth. The surname McDonald, however, suggests a daughter of Edward McDonald, an early settler on the Roanoke with whom William's father Malcolm Campbell had an account for tanning in 1748 (see above). Edward Campbell and his wife Mary had four daughters. One of them was indeed named Rebecca but the

---

[31] Ibid.

eldest was named Elizabeth, born in 1753. This would be an appropriate time frame to be the spouse of William Campbell, himself born around 1750, and whose eldest child was born in 1773. It would also be an interesting family conjunction given the storied rivalry between Campbells and McDonalds in western Scotland, although it has been pointed out that marriages between Campbells and McDonalds in Scotland were (and remain) quite common.[32]

William Campbell had three sons by his first wife Elizabeth: Thomas, Archibald (whom I shall call Archibald Campbell the younger), and John. William Campbell the elder would divorce Elizabeth in a rather spectacular case in 1779, and married Susannah Dabney in 1781. William and Susannah then had four children: William (whom I shall call William Campbell junior[33]), James, Rhoda, and Polly (all of these four born after 1781).

**Family of William Campbell (ca. 1750 - 1804)**

m. Elizabeth McDonald (?) ca. 1772
m. Susannah Dabney in 1781

**Thomas Campbell**  b. ca. 1770

**Archibald Campbell**  b. ca. 1770

**John Campbell**  b. ca. 1777

---

[32] Marion Campbell, *Argyll: The Enduring Heartland* (Grantown-on-Spey, Scotland: Baxter Photography, second edition revised, 1995), p. 39.

[33] Because he was the son of another William Campbell. I have called Archibald Campbell, the son of William Campbell, "the younger."

William Campbell   b. ca. 1781

James Campbell   b. ca. 1783

Rhoda Campbell   b. ca. 1784

Polly Campbell   b. ca. 1786

In 1770, the portion of Augusta County in which William Campbell the elder was living was incorporated into the newly formed Botetourt County. In 1773 William Campbell the elder was licensed to keep an "ordinary," that is a store, in his home.

On March 11, 1774, William's brother Archibald Campbell the elder died without immediate family, and his will granted his plantation to Thomas Campbell, William's oldest son. Archibald granted other properties to his brother William and to Archibald and John Simpson, the sons of his sister Elizabeth (Campbell) Simpson (see the summary of this will in the "Historical Documents section below, Item 2).[34]

William Campbell the elder would have been about twenty-five years of age when the American Revolutionary War began but we do not know what role he may have played in the War. He is not to be confused with another William Campbell of Augusta County known as one of the heroes of the Battle of Kings Mountain in the Revolutionary War and for whom Campbell County, Virginia, was named.[35]

---

[34] Botetourt County, Virginia, Will Book A, p. 78. See the full text of this will in the Historical Documents section below, Item 2.

[35] General William Campbell, famous for his role in the Battle of Kings Mountain, died in 1781. His wife's name was Elizabeth, but she was Elizabeth Henry, the sister of American Patriot Patrick Henry.

As mentioned above, William Campbell the elder divorced his first wife Elizabeth in 1779. An account quoting contemporary court records is given in a work on the history of Roanoke, Virginia:

> There is the case ... of Elizabeth Campbell, who sued her husband William, declaring that the "cruel monster ... drove her from her House and Home, and almost Naked and without a shilling". He even had separated her from her infants, "which were her only Consolation and Comfort". Had it not been for friends, she would have continued naked and unfed. She went on to say that, though she had given no provocation whatsoever, William threatened to take her life and had beaten, stamped, and abused her with "Instruments of Iron in the most cruel, savage, and barbarous and outrageous manner. William, defending himself, replied in sentimental vein "that at the celebration of his nuptials he flattered himself with having taken an agreable [sic] companion, whose happiness he was desirous of preserving". It turned out, however, that Elizabeth, "Lazy and Disobedient to her Husband's Commands, was addicted to getting Drunk". He declared that her "Enormous Crimes" were sufficient to justify his treatment of her", which were not so Cruel, Sav[ag]e, and Barbarous as she had set forth in her Bill, nor as she deserves. He argued that a husband had every right to punish a wife who "should exceed the lines of decency". Colonel William Fleming, William McClanahan, and Robert Poage, who composed the committee to which the case was submitted, allowed Elizabeth for her separate maintenance one-fifth of her husband's estate, amounting to £ 1,127. Soon thereafter

William married a woman by the name of Susanna Dabney.³⁶

William Campbell married Susannah Dabney in 1781. They had a large household at the Great Lick and apparently the sons from William's earlier marriage to Elizabeth continued to live with their father. An "enumeration" (census) of Botetourt County in 1785 shows two persons named William Campbell in different districts of the county. The household of one of them contained three persons; the other contained eight persons with one dwelling and two other buildings and the latter is almost certainly William Campbell the elder since by this time he had six children. Polly may not have been born at the time this census was taken. In addition to the parents and children, William Campbell's will would specifically mention three slaves—Amey, Dingo, and Daniel—who were part of the William Campbell estate.

William Campbell's sister Elizabeth (not to be confused his first wife Elizabeth) had married William Simpson but some time before 1789 William Simpson died leaving their sons Archibald Simpson and John Simpson fatherless. In 1789 William Campbell the elder was appointed the guardian of Archibald Simpson. In the next year he paid Archibald Simpson, now in his guardianship, £ 46 for a tract of land on Long Lick that William the elder's brother Archibald the elder had granted to Archibald Simpson in his 1774 will. Ar-

---

[36] Charlotte Temple, *Roanoke: Story of County and City* (Works Progress Administration Writers Project; Roanoke: Roanoke City School Board, 1942), pp. 50-51.

chibald Simpson would later migrate to Tennessee along with William Campbell (elder)'s son Archibald Campbell (the younger).

On November 4, 1799, William Campbell the elder made out his will. This will granted money but no property to his son Thomas, who had inherited the plantation of William Campbell's brother Archibald. It granted money to his daughters Rhoda and Polly and a saddle and bridle to each of them. He left his wife his household effects and two slaves. Susannah was named executrix of the will along with Matthew Pate, who owned a mill near the Great Lick.[37]

William Campbell's will indicates something of his Protestant beliefs and probably his specifically Presbyterian piety:

> In the name of God Amen I William Campbell of Botetourt County being sick & weak of Body, but in perfect Senses & memory of mind do make ordain constitute & appoint this my last will and Testament in the manner & form following (viz) First I give my soul to Almighty God hoping and trusting in Jesus Christ for life & Justification Secondly I give my Body to the Earth from whence it was taken to be buried in a desent [sic] manner without pomp or vanity according to the discretion of my Executor...[38]

The will reveals an extent of property—"my worldly Estate which it hath pleased God to bless me with"—

---

[37] Will of William Campbell, Botetourt County, Virginia, Will Book B, pp. 56-57. The full text of this will is given in item 3 in the Historical Documents section below.

[38] Botetourt County, Virginia, Will Book B, p. 56.

that makes William Campbell easily the wealthiest man in the lineage given here. The earlier assessment around 1779 that his previous wife was to receive £ 1,127, implies that the court assessed his total estate as being worth more than £ 5,600, a very substantial estate on the eighteenth-century Virginia frontier. The various provisions of the will also imply that William anticipated a substantial "worldly Estate" to be divided by his heirs (see the text of this will in the "Historical Documents section below, Item 3).

The will also reveals that William Campbell was a slaveholder, and so far as I know, the only slaveholder in the lineage of Campbell families given here. His brother Archibald Campbell the Elder also owned slaves.[39] William mentioned three slaves by name in his will: Daniel, Amey, and Dingo. Amey and Dingo were a married couple; Daniel may have been their son. The will made provision for other slaves to be purchased for his children when they came to maturity. Amey and Dingo also appeared in a later enumeration of the estate of William Campbell.[40]

The 1799 will of William Campbell the elder specified that the proceeds of his estate were to be used to acquire "Land in the Western Country's [sic] to be purchased by my Executors" for four of his five sons: Archibald, William (junior), James and John. The amounts of land were specified as 200 acres for Archibald and 400 acres each for William, James, and John.

---

[39] See the will of Archibald Campbell the elder in the Historical Documents section below, Item 2.

[40] Botetourt County, Virginia, Will Book B, p. 200.

Each of the latter three boys (that is, excluding Archibald) was also willed a slave or funds with which they might purchase a slave and a saddle and bridle for each of them.

I do not know why the next-oldest son Archibald was granted half of the amount of land to be purchased and was excluded from the provision of horse, saddle, and bridle and funds to purchase a slave. Perhaps, like his older brother Thomas, he had already inherited some funds or property. In fact, when William Campbell stipulated at the conclusion of his will that the remaining property was to be divided between his heirs, he specified that the estate was to be divided between "my five children (viz) William, James, John, Rhoda, and Polly," again excluding Thomas and Archibald. This could be because they were the children of his first wife Elizabeth although so far as we know John was also the child of Elizabeth. It might simply mean, as suggested above, that the older two sons had already inherited substantial property.

The expression "the Western Country"[41] in this will could be interpreted as denoting Kentucky, which lay immediately to the west of Virginia and which was in fact included in the early boundaries of Botetourt County. But expressions like this had also been used to denote the "western country" very broadly. For example, an account of the Methodist Episcopal Church itinerant minister William McKendree (later a bishop) indicates that in the year 1800 he was "appointed presiding

---

41 In two first two instances in the will the wording seems to be "Western Country's," and in the latter instances "Western Country."

elder for all the western country, comprehending in his district the whole of Kentucky and part of three other states, viz: Ohio, Virginia and Tennessee."[42] Similarly, a Virginia will of 1806 specified that land should be sold by the executors and then new land purchased for heirs "either in the state of Kentucky, or some other part of the western country that my executors may think will be most to the general interest of my heirs."[43] The expression "the Western Country," then, could be interpreted very broadly.

The will stipulated that William Campbell the elder's wife Susannah was to be provided for on the property purchased by his son John and we know that John Campbell elected to remain in the part of Botetourt County which became Roanoke County and the City of Roanoke. John was buried in the Fairview Cemetery in Roanoke after he died in 1863. By his 1799 will, then, William Campbell the elder recognized that some of his sons would want to take part in the westward expansion of the US population beyond the Appalachians that was beginning in his time and his will allowed that at least four of his sons would have the option of finding and purchasing land "in the Western Country."

William Campbell the elder died in 1804 and his will was probated in that year. His wife Susannah appears in a census of Botetourt County taken in 1810,

---

[42] Lewis Collins, *Historical Sketches of Kentucky* (Maysville, KY: Lewis Collins, 1848), p. 130.

[43] The will of Lewis Ashby, Frederick county, Virginia, made on the 20th of March, 1806; in Conway Robinson, ed., *Reports of Cases Decided in the Supreme Court of Appeals and in the General Court of Virginia* (Richmond: J. E. Goode, printer; vol. 1; second edition, n.d.), p. 60.

which shows her living with one son between the ages of 25 and 45 and one daughter in the same age range. This probably refers to her son John Campbell since the will of her husband had specified that she was to live with John after her husband's death. The daughter may have been her youngest, Polly, who married a man named Simon Camper in July of 1810.

The 1810 census of Botetourt County has no reference to heads of households named Thomas Campbell, Archibald Campbell, or James Campbell. There is one reference to a William Campbell whose age range would fit that of William Campbell junior who remained in Botetourt County.

The 1820 census for Botetourt County lists no William Campbell, no Thomas Campbell, no Archibald Campbell, no John Campbell, no James Campbell. In fact, no persons named Campbell appear in Botetourt County. This is a bit of a mystery because we should have expected at least John Campbell and probably William to show up in this census. The 1830 census ten years later does show a William Campbell in Botetourt County whose age (between 40 and 50 years old with a wife of the same age) could correspond to William junior. Three persons named John Campbell appear in this census and we know that John Campbell the son of William Campbell the elder remained there. But in 1830 there is no reference to Archibald Campbell, James Campbell, or Thomas Campbell in Botetourt County.

By 1840 Roanoke County had been created from the region of Botetourt County including the Great Lick where the family of William Campbell the elder had lived. The census of that year shows two persons named William Campbell in what remained of Botetourt County, but no one named William Campbell in Roanoke County. This is consistent with the fact that William Campbell the younger lived in Botetourt County. The 1840 census showed no persons named James, Archibald, or Thomas Campbell in either Botetourt or Roanoke counties.

Where had these Campbells gone? John Campbell remained in Botetourt, then Roanoke County. William Campbell remained in Botetourt County. Thomas, Archibald, and James never appeared there after 1800.

The most obvious explanation is that some of the Campbell sons took up their father's challenge to find land in "the Western Country." I cannot trace what happened to Thomas and James, but Archibald Campbell (the younger), along with his first cousin Archibald Simpson and his half-sister Rhoda Campbell, went to Tennessee.

## Chapter 3
## Tennessee

The State of Tennessee was created in 1796 from the western territories of North Carolina. Tennessee played a crucial role in the westward expansion of the United States. Andrew Jackson, who would serve as the first president of the United States from a region west of the Appalachians, had been part of the Tennessee constitutional convention of 1796 and he came to represent the aspirations of frontier people. The home he acquired in 1804, the Hermitage, is in eastern Davidson County just a few miles west of Wilson County where our Campbells would settle.

The new state of Tennessee inherited some county divisions from North Carolina: Davidson County, which includes present-day Nashville, had been created in 1783, and in 1786 Sumner County was created from eastern portions of Davidson County. Three years after Tennessee statehood, Wilson County was created, less than two weeks before William Campbell the elder signed his will in Virginia. When created on October 26, 1799, Wilson County consisted of the parts of Sumner County south of the Cumberland River. Some earlier property transactions of Davidson County and then Sumner County refer to land that was to become Wilson County.

The area that became Wilson County, Tennessee, was settled beginning around 1799 in communities associated with local waterways. Historical accounts refer to these settlements as "creek communities" and among the earliest were communities on Round Lick and Smith's Fork.[44] The Round Lick community would eventually become the site of Watertown, Tennessee, a settlement that included many of the early Campbell pioneers described here. Round Lick is several miles south of Lebanon, the county seat, and Smith's Fork is about eight miles farther south of it. Some of the Campbells would own property in the Smith's Fork settlement which was eventually called Statesville, Tennessee, and is just a few miles north of the Cannon County line.

Campbell and other Scottish family names appear in abundance in early records of Wilson County, and many early settlers came by way of Virginia as well as North Carolina and other eastern states. There are numerous Campbells in these early records, some of whom bear the names of the Botetourt County, Virginia, Campbells. Family researchers have had to sort carefully through these names. There was, for example, a William Campbell who received one of the earliest of North Carolina grants to Tennessee property along with a Gus Cathey (or "Cathy") who in 1789 paid taxes on a grant of 640 acres on the south side of the Cumberland River in what became Wilson County. This William Campbell appears in early tax rolls in Wilson County as owning 266 acres (apparently his portion of the original grant) on Spencer Creek. But he was not likely to be William Campbell junior, who was born in Virginia

---

[44] James V. Drake, *Historical Sketch of Wilson County, Tennessee, From Its First Settlement to the Present Time* (Nashville: Tavel, Eastman & Howell, 1879), in section on "Pioneer Settlers."

around 1780 and thus would have been a child when this William Campbell and Gus Cathey acquired their property.

The first person to appear in Wilson County whom we can link to Botetourt County, Virginia, was Archibald Simpson, the nephew and ward of William Campbell the elder. As we have seen, William Campbell had been appointed as Archibald Simpson's guardian. On March 4, 1801, Archibald Simpson purchased 140 acres in the Round Lick community from a John Irvin. On the same date a John Curry purchased 250 acres from Irvin and this land was also in the Round Lick community. On April 30 of that year, Simpson sold 23 acres of this land but purchased an additional 18 acres from John Curry. These negotiations left Archibald Simpson with 135 acres in Wilson County.

Archibald Simpson married a Mary Curry in Wilson County, Tennessee, in the same year and it is natural to assume that she was the daughter of this John Curry. Both were setting up homesteads on Round Lick at the same time. Early tax lists in Wilson County show Archibald Simpson paying taxes on 135 acres on Round Lick for every year between 1803 and 1807 although I would note that in the 1806 entry the name Archibald was abbreviated as "Archel."[45]

## Archibald and Rebecca (Jacobs) Campbell

In 1804 an "Archel" Campbell appears in early Wilson County tax lists, in 1805 "Arch" Campbell, and

---

[45] *Tax Lists of Wilson County, Tennessee, 1803-1807*, pp. 11. 19, 48, 90, and 133.

in 1807 "Archibald" Campbell. All these references are to an individual in the Round Lick community.[46] Given the one-time spelling of Archibald Simpson's name as "Archel" and the fact that these are all in the same area, it seems likely that they refer to the same Archibald Campbell. There is good reason to see this Archibald Campbell as the son of William Campbell the elder of Virginia, that is, Archibald Campbell the younger who was the first cousin of Archibald Simpson.

These references between 1804 and 1807 to Archibald Campbell show him as not owning property and suggest that Archibald Campbell the younger may not have yet received the money provided for land in his father's will, which was not probated until 1804 and was not inventoried until 1806. On the other hand, Archibald Campbell sold 30 acres on Round Lick to Edward Jacobs in 1820[47] and I have not seen a deed of purchase for this land though he must have acquired it between 1807 and 1820.

Archibald Campbell appears consistently in records placing him in the Round Lick community from 1804 and in federal census records in Wilson County from 1820 through 1860, listing his birthplace as Virginia in 1850 and 1860 when the census began to ask about the birthplace of those who were enumerated. In the 1820 census his name is given as "Arthur" Campbell, but misspellings of the name Archibald are legion:

---

[46] *Tax Lists of Wilson County, Tennessee, 1803-1807*, pp. 18, 47, 119. I do not know why he does not appear in 1806.

[47] Thomas E. Partlow, ed. *Wilson County Deed Books* (Easley, SC: Southern Historical Press, 1984), p. 166.

it sometimes appears as "Arch," "Archie," "Archel" (as we have seen above with both him and Archibald Simpson), "Archabald," "Archebald," or "Aschabald," and it is easy to see how a mistaken or careless census taker could write the more common name "Arthur" in place of it. The identification of his children and the proximity of his record to that of Edward G. Jacobs through several census records as well as the lack of any other "Arthur" Campbell in earlier or later records all indicate that this is the same person.

The fact that this Archibald Campbell appears in the same community as Archibald Simpson from Botetourt County, Virginia, is one reason for connecting him to the Botetourt County Campbells. It suggests that Archibald Campbell may have followed his first cousin, who had lived with his own family as a brother, to Tennessee. Perhaps Archibald Campbell traveled with Archibald Simpson when he first came to Tennessee. But in February, 1807, Archibald Simpson sold his 135 acres on Round Lick to John Alexander. He may have moved to Bedford County, Tennessee, for a while, but he eventually settled in Gibson County, Indiana.[48]

Another connection between Archibald Campbell and the Campbells of Botetourt County, Virginia, involves the tragic figure of Rhody Campbell. On January 30, 1819, a marriage was recorded in Wilson County, Tennessee, between Rhody Campbell and Elisha Winters. But Elisha died in June of the same year, and his "non-cuperative" (death-bed, oral) will was witnessed

---

[48] Archibald Simpson appears on US census reports in Gibson County, Indiana, from 1820.

by Archibald Campbell, Rebecca Campbell, and Patsy Campbell.[49] I do not know who Patsy Campbell was, but the name "Rhody" Campbell suggests Rhoda Campbell, the half-sister of Archibald Campbell the younger and the cousin of Archibald Simpson from Botetourt County, Virginia. The fact that Archibald Campbell and his wife Rebecca witnessed this death-bed scene suggests a close relationship.

Three years later, Rhody was again married, this time as Rhody Winters, to an Ambrose Holland on March 16, 1822. I do not know where Ambrose Holland came from or where he went—perhaps he died—but Rhody was yet again married on December 28, 1824, this time as Rhody Holland, to a James Cropper. Cropper did the best job of surviving a marriage to Rhody Winters Holland née Campbell, leaving her a widow in 1848 after 24 years of marriage. In 1850 she appeared in the census of Wilson County as a widow, born in Virginia, age 69 and thus born around 1781, when William Campbell the elder had married Susannah Dabney. Rhody died of whooping cough in 1860 at the age of 79.[50]

At some time around 1805 Archibald Campbell married a woman from North Carolina named Rebecca though we do not have a marriage record for them. Family records supported by consistent evidence sug-

---

[49] Thomas E. Partlow, ed., *Wilson County, Tennessee Wills: Books 1-13, 1802-1850* (Easley, SC: Southern Historical Press, 1981), p. 12.

[50] Ron V. Jackson, ed., *U.S. Federal Census Mortality Schedules Index* (database on-line; Provo, UT: The Generations Network, Inc., 1999), ID # MRT197_72613.

gest that Archibald Campbell's wife Rebecca was Rebecca Jacobs, the daughter of Edward G. Jacobs, a Revolutionary War soldier and originally a Maryland resident who had moved to North Carolina and then to Tennessee and whose homestead was listed next to that of Archibald and Rebecca Campbell in Wilson County through several decades. The connection to Edgar G. Jacobs signals the beginning of a long connection between the Campbells and the Jacob (or "Jacobs") and Gaither families of Maryland, for a son of Archibald and Rebecca Campbell in our Campbell line would marry a Gaither woman from the same Maryland family that had moved to Tennessee.

We now need to take a little excursion back in time to pick up the narrative of Edward G. Jacobs and his daughter Rebecca who was to marry Archibald Campbell. Edgar Gaither Jacobs was born in Sugarloaf, Frederick County[51] in colonial Maryland, on January 4, 1759, the son of Marylanders Jeremiah Jacob[52] (1712-1781) and Rachel Gaither (1718-1781). He would have been 17 years old at the outbreak of the American Revolution and he served at the rank of private in the Maryland Militia in the Revolutionary War under a Captain Brisco and Colonel John Mordock.

---

[51] Some sources have Montgomery County, Maryland, but Montgomery County was not formed (from Frederick County) until 1776.

[52] The name "Jacob" (without the terminal "s") appears consistently for Jeremiah Jacob; the spelling "Jacobs" (with terminal "s") appears consistently for his son Edward Gaither Jacobs except for one Wilson County, Tennessee, census record in which his name is given as "Jacob."

Edward Gaither Jacobs had a sister, Rebecca Jacob, who had been born on October 1, 1758, in Anne Arundel County, Maryland. She married William Summers, Jr., on October 1, 1778, but Rebecca died on the 25th of June 1779.[53] Five years later, Edward Jacobs would name a daughter Rebecca (or "Rebeckah"), perhaps remembering his deceased sister.

On October 28, 1779, Edward G. Jacobs married Mary Summers (b. 1759) in newly created Montgomery County, Maryland. Shortly after their marriage they moved to Rowan County, North Carolina, along with Jacobs' father Jeremiah Jacob and other family members. In North Carolina, Jacobs apparently re-enlisted, serving in the North Carolina Militia under Captains Nighton and Caldwell. His father Jeremiah Jacob died in Rowan County, North Carolina, in 1781, leaving in his will the 150-acre plot on which he had lived to his son Edward Gaither Jacobs though requiring payment of £ 300 and eight shillings for the land.[54]

Edward Jacobs and his wife lived in this area for almost twenty years until about 1799, although the area where they lived became part of the newly created Iredell County in 1788. Several children were born to them in North Carolina including Samuel Austin (b. 1780),

---

[53] Some accounts state that Rebecca Jacobs Summers died in Iredell County, North Carolina. The county had not yet been created, although it is possible that she and other members of the Jacob family had already moved to North Carolina ahead of her brother Edward Gaither Jacobs, or perhaps Edward G. Jacobs simply returned to Maryland to marry Mary Summers.

[54] Will of Jeremiah Jacob in Rowan County, North Carolina. The will was made out on 10 March 1781.

Jerimiah (Jeremiah, b. 1781), Rebeckah (Rebecca, born on December 15, 1784), Mary S. (presumably Mary Summers, b. 1786), John (b. 1788), Ary (b. 1792), Brazzel (b. 1792), Elizabeth (b. 1793), and Tobinah (b. 1796).

In 1799 the Jacobs family moved westward to settle on the Clinch River in Knox County, Tennessee.[55] Two children were born in this area: a daughter Nancy (b. 1799) and a son Amos (b. 1801).

In about 1803, the family moved once again, this time to Wilson County in central Tennessee, settling in the Round Lick community. Edward G. Jacobs is listed as one of the founding settlers of the Round Lick community. A son who was named Edward Gaither Jacobs, Jr., was born in Wilson County in 1803.

Shortly after his move to Wilson County, I believe that his daughter Rebecca married Archibald Campbell who had only very recently moved to Wilson County, Tennessee, from Botetourt County, Virginia. In subsequent census reports, the homesteads of Edward G. Jacobs and Archibald and Rebecca Campbell are shown as being very close, usually within one or two enumerated households of each other. They also exchanged land with each other: on 8 March 1820 Archibald Campbell sold 30 acres on Round Lick to Edward G. Jacobs.

On June 27, 1833, in Rutherford County, Tennessee, Jacobs applied for a pension as a Revolutionary War soldier, stating he was aged 73 on January 4, 1833.

---

[55] Knox county had been created as a county of North Carolina in 1792, and became part of the state of Tennessee when the latter was created in 1796.

His pension began on November 19 of that year. He died sometime before 1848.

We return now to our narrative of Edward G. Jacobs' daughter Rebecca, who I believe to have married Archibald Campbell sometime around 1804, that is, about a year after the Jacobs' arrival in Wilson County. Archibald and Rebecca Campbell had at least four children between 1804 and 1815: Edward Gaston Campbell (about 1806), Thomas Campbell (1807), Archibald (or "Archabald") Campbell, Jr. (about 1815), and Amos Campbell (about 1815).

**Family of Archibald Campbell (ca. 1770 - 1871)**

m. Rebecca Jacobs ca. 1804

Edward Gaston Campbell  b. ca. 1806

Thomas Campbell  b. 1807

Archibald Campbell, Jr.  b. ca. 1815

Amos Campbell  b. ca. 1815

Public records of Wilson County, Tennessee, show Archibald Campbell engaged in buying and selling land and in jury appearances in the 1820s and beyond. We do not have records of his initial purchases of land in the county but we know that he held land there, since he had begun to sell it by 1820, when he sold 30 acres (noted above) to his father-in-law Edward G. Jacobs. In 1824 Archibald Campbell purchased ten additional acres on the headwaters of Round Lick.[56] In March, 1826, the Sheriff of Wilson County issued a summons to Archibald Campbell to appear before the justices to give testimony on behalf of the state in the case of the State of Tennessee vs. Burton Medglin.[57] A tax list from 1828 shows Archibald Campbell as owning 150 acres on Round Lick and it also shows Edward G. Jacobs with the 30 acres that Archibald had sold him eight years earlier.[58] In 1829 he purchased 31 acres on Round Lick, and in 1830 an additional 30 acres.[59]

On March 18, 1836, Archibald Campbell sold a very substantial 230 acres of land on Round Lick Creek to William Paul and an additional 65 acres to James Gaddy on the same date.[60] Eight days later he purchased a 100-acre plot from William L. Sypert.[61] All of this property was in the vicinity of Round Lick. Twenty

---

[56] Land Entry Book 1824-1845 of Wilson County, Tennessee, p. 49 (p. 22 of original land entry book), and Surveyors Plat Book 1824-1830 of Wilson County, Tennessee, p. 10 (pp. 122-123 of original plat book).

[57] Wilson County, Tennessee, County Court Loose Papers, box 10, folder 3 (on microfilm; I have a photocopy of the document).

[58] In Thomas E. Partlow, ed., *Wilson County, Tennessee, Genealogical Resource Materials 1827-1869* (Greenville, SC: Southern Historical Press, 1997), p. 215. Edward Jacobs (30 acres) is shown on the next page (p. 216).

[59] *Land Entry Book 1824-1845* of Wilson County, Tennessee, pp. 82 and 86.

[60] In Thomas E. Partlow, *Wilson County, Tennessee, Deed Books N-Z, 1829-1853* (Easley, SC: Southern Historical Press, Inc., 1984), pp. 386-387 of original deed books, in Partlow, p. 104; and deed book pp. 387-388, in Partlow, p. 104.

[61] In original deed book, p. 385; in Partlow, *Wilson County, Tennessee, Deed Books N-Z, 1829-1853*, p. 104).

years later the 100-acre plot would be conveyed to his son Archibald Campbell, Jr. (see below).

Through the 1820s, 1830s, and the early 1840s the sons of Archibald and Rebecca Campbell were growing up and eventually establishing families of their own. Edward Gaston Campbell married Arsenath C. Maxwell in Wilson County on December 21, 1827. On January 20, 1840, Thomas Campbell married Anna (or "Annie") Gaither in newly created Cannon County, to the south of Wilson County (see the next section). In 1842, Archibald Campbell, Jr., would marry Anna's sister Mary Ann Gaither in Wilson County, and in the same year Amos Campbell married Nancy Belt in Wilson County.

As we shall see, Thomas and Anna Campbell moved in the 1840s to Cannon County where Anna's Gaither family had settled. On February 14, 1854, Archibald Campbell (Sr.) deeded his 100-acre plot on Round Lick Creek to his son Archibald Campbell, Jr., on the condition that the younger Archibald would provide for the upkeep of Archibald (Sr.) and Rebecca Campbell in their old age: "for the further consideration of his providing for me & my wife Rebecca Campbell a home and good comfortable food clothes & lodging and the taking good care of us in sickness or in health during our natural life and at my death & wife's death..." (see the text of this deed in the Historical Documents section, Item 4).[62]

---

[62] Deed from Archibald Campbell, Sr., to Archibald Campbell, Jr., dated 13 February 1854, in Wilson County, Tennessee, Deed Book A#2 p. 68; from microfilm.

Rebecca (Jacobs) Campbell must have died at some point between 1854 and 1860, for the 1860 census shows Archibald Campbell living with the family of Stephen and Elizabeth Griffin. Elizabeth (Jacobs) Griffin was a younger sister of Rebecca (Jacobs) Campbell who had been born in 1793. She had married Stephen Griffin on October 4, 1839, in Wilson County. The 1850 census had shown another Jacobs sister, Nancy Jacobs (b. 1799 in Knox County, Tennessee), living with Stephen and Elizabeth (Jacobs) Griffin. So it is understandable that after the death of Rebecca (Jacobs) Campbell, Archibald would live with the family of Rebecca's sister Elizabeth and her husband Stephen Griffin.

What is sad, though, if one knows the earlier history, is that the 1860 census also shows the family of Archibald Campbell, Jr., and his wife Mary Ann (Gaither) Campbell living nearby in Wilson County. Archibald Campbell, Sr., was not living with them despite the fact that the elder Archibald Campbell had granted land to Archibald Jr. on the condition that Archibald Jr. would provide for him in his old age. Apparently the scenario for his old age that Archibald Campbell, Sr., had envisioned with his son Archibald Campbell, Jr., had gone awry. We know that within a few years Archibald Campbell, Jr., and Mary Ann (Gaither) Campbell would move to Illinois. Perhaps they had already made a decision to do so and were preparing for their move in 1860. At some point after 1860, Archibald Campbell, Sr., would move to Cannon County to live with his son Thomas Campbell. One wonders if this move was related in any way to the beginning of the Civil War: Archibald and Mary Ann Campbell would have been moving from a southern state to a northern state in the midst of the war. Archibald Campbell, Sr., would die in Cannon County in 1771, and it is to the story of his son Thomas Campbell that we now turn.

**Thomas and Anna (Gaither)**
**and Pernetia (Witherspoon/Armstrong) Campbell**

Thomas Campbell[63] was born in June, 1807, in Wilson County, Tennessee, the second child of Archibald and Rebecca Campbell. He had grown up in the Round Lick community with his parents and three brothers.

Smith's Fork, now Statesville, Tennessee

Thomas Campbell purchased land on Smith's Fork in the early 1830s in the vicinity of present Statesville, Tennessee, six or seven miles south of his father's property on Round Lick Creek and eight to ten miles

---

[63] Thomas Campbell's name is often given in genealogical records as Thomas Edward Campbell, but I have as yet seen no evidence of the middle name Edward.

north of the present Cannon County line.[64] We do not know that he ever occupied this property, however. It may have been acquired as farmland.

As we have seen above, Thomas Campbell and his brother Archibald Campbell, Jr., married sisters Anna and Mary Ann Gaither, daughters of Edward and Mary (Dyson) Gaither of Cannon County. Anna Gaither had been born in North Carolina in 1822, probably in either Rowan County (where her parents were married) or Iredell County just to the west of Rowan County. The family had migrated to Tennessee in the late 1820s or early 1830s. Anna Gaither and Thomas Campbell in fact shared a pair of great-grandparents, for Anna's father Edward Gaither was a descendant of Rachel Gaither and Jeremiah Jacob, as was Thomas Campbell's mother Rebecca Jacobs. The Jacob (Jacobs) and Gaither families, then, had migrated together from Maryland to North Carolina and from there to the same part of Tennessee. The little town of Statesville, Tennessee (formerly the Smith's Fork community), was named for Statesville, North Carolina, the county seat of Iredell County, North Carolina, from which many of these early settlers had come.

Thomas and Anna Campbell were married on Tuesday, January 21, 1840, in Cannon County and they moved to live in Cannon County at some point in the 1840s, almost certainly in the area on Locke's Creek

---

[64] A land record for Wilson County, Tennessee, records "James Campbell to Thomas Campbell 45 acres on Smith's Fork for $200" (deed book p. 401); in Thomas E. Partlow, ed., *Wilson County, Tennessee Deed Books N-Z, 1829-1853* (Easley, SC: Southern Historical Press, Inc., 1984), p. 49.

where Thomas would eventually establish a homestead. The Gaither home was nearby. After their marriage in 1840 they had five children: Mahala ("Mahaly"), Mary, John, Amos, and Buson.

**Family of Thomas Campbell**

m. Anna Gaither in 1840

m. Pernetia Witherspoon Armstrong in 1851

**Mahala Campbell** b. 1840

**Mary Ann Campbell** b. 1842

**John Watson Campbell** b. 1845

**Amos Dison Campbell** b. 1847

**Buson Campbell** b. 1848 (died as infant)

Thomas Campbell's wife Anna (or "Annie") Campbell died in September 1849 in Cannon County, and their ten-month-old son Buson died in November of that year, both of a disease identified as "flux" (probably dysentery) in a subsequent mortality survey.[65] In February 1851 Thomas Campbell married a widow Pernetia (or "Pernisia") Armstrong whose maiden name was Witherspoon. In 1856 Anna Campbell's father Edward Gaither died in Cannon County,

---

[65] On p. 49 of of the original survey; in Helen C. and Timothy R. Marsh, eds., *1850 Mortality Schedule of Tennessee* (Shelbyville, Tennessee: Marsh Historical Collection, 1982), p. 16: "Anna Campbell, age 27 F. Married, b. in N.C. died in Nov (1849) of "Flux," ill for 21 days". The next entry is "Buson Campbell, age 10m b. Tenn., died in Nov. (1849) of Flux; ill for 8 days." Anna's death date is given as September 18, 1849 in the family Bible of her son John Watson Campbell (she is called "Annie" Campbell in that Bible): *Maury County Cousins*, p. 453.

and his will designated both his daughter Mary Ann Campbell (who had married Archibald Campbell, Jr.) and the "heirs of Anna Campbell" as beneficiaries. In the next year, Thomas Campbell acquired property in Cannon County from an Edward Gaither, perhaps this means from the estate of the deceased Edward Gaither.

At some point in the 1860s, before 1866 when he made out his will, the very elderly Archibald Campbell, Sr., came to live in Cannon County with his son Thomas. This may have been during the period of the Civil War. Archibald Campbell is listed in the 1870 census with Thomas' family giving his age as 108 (somewhat fancifully, I'm inclined to think). Archibald Campbell died soon after, probably in early 1871, leaving his inheritance entirely to Thomas and explicitly disinheriting other claimants. Amos Gaither, brother of Thomas Campbell's first wife Anna, served as one of the witnesses to the will (see the abstract of this will in the Historical Documents section, Item 6).

Thomas Campbell home on Locke's Creek Road, Cannon County, Tennessee (ca. 1986)

Thomas Campbell's home in Cannon County was on the east side of Locke's Creek Road which follows Locke's Creek north from the old Mufreesboro-

Woodbury Pike (the old route of US Highway 70S). The home is still standing there, and has been added to substantially since Thomas Campbell built it in the 1840s or 1850s. The original structure was probably a log cabin.

In 1868 Thomas Campbell became the guardian of the younger children of Allen Morgan (see the text of this document in the Historical Documents section, Item 7).[66] Allen Morgan (his full name was John Allen Morgan) was apparently a very close friend. Two of Thomas Campbell's sons would marry daughters of Allen Morgan, and Thomas named his last son Morgan. The name "Allen" became a beloved middle name in the Campbell family and has been passed down through several successive generations of Campbell men.

Thomas Campbell made out his own will on March 4, 1886, and died two days later. His will was not signed but was marked, which often indicates a person who did not know how to write. His will was probated on March 8th in the next year, 1887. An "R. F. Gaither" was a witness to the will. This will provided that his sons John W. and Amos Campbell were to sell all of his lands except for an apple orchard and distribute the funds between themselves and their sisters. The apple orchard was to be sold separately with the proceeds to be used by his wife as long as she lived (see the text of this will in the Historical Documents section below, Item 8).

---

[66] Guardianship bond, recorded in Cannon County, 8 October 1868 (1854-1872, film #12, page 462).

## John Watson and Serecia Emalina (Morgan) and Frances Parilee (Tenpenny) Campbell

John Watson Campbell was born in 1845, the eldest son of Thomas and Anna Campbell. He had grown up in the Campbell homestead on Locke's Creek Road. His occupation is shown as "farmer" in all census records between 1870 and 1910.[67] John Watson and his younger brother Amos Campbell married sisters Serecia and Serena Morgan, respectively, the daughters of the Allen Morgan mentioned above.

The Readyville Mill, built ca. 1870
near Locke's Creek Road,
Cannon County, Tennessee

After their father's death in 1887 and the division of Thomas Campbell's property, John W. Campbell's brother Amos Campbell purchased the Thomas Camp-

---

[67] 1870 census for Cannon County, Tennessee, district no 1, page 2; 1880 census for Cannon County, Tennessee, page 2a; 1900 census for Warren County, Tennessee, p. 5b; 1910 census for Maury County, Tennessee, sheet 2.

bell homestead on Locke's Creek Road and continued to live there. A photograph shows Amos and his wife Serena Campbell in front of the homestead with their dog named "Old Forrest" for Civil War General (and founder of the Ku Klux Klan) Nathan Bedford Forrest.

Serecia (or "Reacy") and John W. Campbell had nine children in the twenty-one year period between 1868 and 1887. Although John Watson Campbell would remarry after the death of Serecia in 1893, Serecia Morgan was the mother of all of his children.

### Family of John Watson Campbell

m. Serecia Emalina Morgan in 1867
m. Frances Parilee Tenpenny in 1893

Rosannah A. Campbell  b. 1868
Albert L. Campbell  b. 1870
James Allen Campbell  b. 1872
Mary Ann Campbell  b. 1875
Serena Callie Campbell  b. 1877
Lydia J. Campbell  b. 1880
Edward Dison Campbell  b. 1882
Nettie A. Campbell  b. 1885
Morgan Thomas Campbell  b. 1887

The recollection of the Campbell family in Tennessee is that John Watson Campbell and his father Thomas Campbell were both Baptists. We do not know when the transition from Presbyterian to Baptist churches occurred; it could have been as early as when Archibald Campbell moved to Tennessee.

In 1893 Serecia died. Later that year John Watson Campbell married Frances Parilee Tenpenny. The Tenpenny family was a well known family in Cannon County who had settled in the same general area as the Campbells on the western edge of the county. A cave that my grandfather remembered playing in as a child is called the Tenpenny Cave for this family. It is off Hollis Creek Road south of the Murfreesboro-Woodbury Pike (now US-70S).

John Watson Campbell
and Frances Tenpenny (his second wife)

For whatever reason, John Watson Campbell does not seem to have been as tied to the family in Cannon County as his brother Amos was. His father had died in 1886, and perhaps after the death of Serecia in 1893 he felt more liberty to move to be with his children. Serecia had died in 1893 in Cannon County and

John Watson Campbell married Frances Parilee Tenpenny in the same year in that county. At some point prior to 1900 John Watson Campbell moved his family to the community of Dibrell in Warren County, Tennessee, about fifteen miles east of Woodbury and ten miles north of McMinnville, the county seat.[68] In the 1910 census, he is shown as living in Lawrence County, Tennessee, with his wife Frances and in the immediate vicinity of his children Albert L. Campbell and Morgan T. Campbell and their families.[69]

At some point after 1910 John Watson Campbell moved yet again to Maury County, Tennessee, following his son Morgan Thomas Campbell, who moved there in the same decade. He died in Maury County in 1915 and is buried at the Arlington Cemetery there. His family Bible, which contains important genealogical information, was handed on to Morgan Thomas Campbell and its family information was subsequently published in a 1969 volume entitled *Maury County Cousins*.[70]

### James Allen and Lillie Ann (Sullivan) Campbell

James Allen Campbell was the third child of John Watson Campbell and Serecia Emalina Morgan. His middle name "Allen" was the first name of his maternal

---

[68] 1900 census for Warren County, Tennessee, p. 5b.

[69] 1910 census for Lawrence County, Tennessee, page 2A; these entries have written in the left-hand margin "Marcella and Brace [Bruce?] Roads." This 1910 census report lists his mother's birthplace as North Carolina. This is correct although in the 1900 census he had listed his mother's birthplace as Tennessee.

[70] *Maury County Cousins* (Maury County, Tennessee: Maury County Historical Society, 1967), pp. 451-453.

grandfather Allen Morgan who was also the close friend of his paternal grandfather. James Allen Campbell was born on the 21st of September, 1872, which would have been a year after the death of his great grandfather Archibald Campbell. When he was thirteen years old, in 1886, his grandfather Thomas Campbell died in Cannon County, Tennessee.

As a young man James Allen Campbell attended Woodbury College in Woodbury, the county seat of Cannon County. Woodbury College had originally been established as the Baptist Female Academy in Woodbury in 1855 but the school became coeducational and in 1868 the Tennessee legislature approved changing the name of the institution to Woodbury College with a further stipulation that no sectarian test would be required for matriculation or in other aspects of the administration of the College.[71] This "college," as many similarly named institutions of its time, provided the equivalent of a high school education for students. Woodbury College would eventually become Woodbury Central High School. A report card for the spring term, 1893, when James Allen Campbell was 20 years old, shows that he made a 99 in written arithmetic, 100 in algebra, 98 in grammar, 96 in rhetoric, and 94 in bookkeeping. He is also listed as making 100 in the general category of "deportment."

---

[71] Act of Tennessee legislature, March 5, 1868, in *Acts of the State of Tennessee Passed at the First Session of the Thirty-Fifth General Assembly for the Years 1867-1868* (Nashville: S. C. Mercer, 1868), p. 165.

At some point in his early life, James Allen Campbell sat for a portrait that is either in pencil or more likely charcoal, a portrait that depicts him as a man of delicate features dressed in a fine suit.

**Portrait of James Allen Campbell**

On March 29, 1894, James Allen Campbell signed a contract with the directors of School District One in Cannon County to serve as a school teacher beginning on the 10th of July, 1895, for which he was to be paid thirty five dollars per month. One of the three directors of the school district who signed the contract was "John Campbell," who could have been John Watson Campbell.[72] A family story that I heard repeated by my

---

[72] Although the 1880 census showed other John Campbells in Cannon County.

grandfather Elam Campbell was that James Campbell taught school in the church building that was to become the Sunny Slope Church of Christ on Hollis Creek Road in western Cannon County. James Allen Campbell paid taxes in Cannon County, Tennessee, for every year between 1894 and 1896, and then paid a poll tax in 1897 in Warren County, where his father and stepmother had settled. He was probably still living with his parents in the Dibrell community in Warren County, then, the year before his own marriage.[73]

James Allen Campbell and Lillie Ann Sullivan applied for a marriage license back in Cannon County on January 22, 1898, and their marriage was solemnized on the next day, Sunday, January 23, 1898, by Justice of the Peace J. T. Jetson. Lillie Ann Sullivan's father was James T. Sullivan (1850-1906), but we know very little about his family. Her mother was Nancy Elizabeth McBroom (1852-1934), the daughter of James McBroom (1827-1870) and Rachel C. Hayes (1832-1906). The McBroom family was a Scots-Irish family that had come to Rowan County, North Carolina, and thence to the part of Tennessee that would become Cannon County. One of Nancy McBroom's great uncles, Henry D. McBroom, was one of the pioneering settlers of the area that became Cannon County, and in fact the county

---

[73] Tax receipts for James Campbell in Cannon County for 1894 (dated January 15, 1895), 1895 (dated January 15, 1896), and 1896 (dated February 27, 1897). Tax receipt for James Campbell in Warren County for 1897 (dated March 26, 1898).

government had been organized in his home in 1836.[74] The particular branch of the McBroom family from which Nancy was descended lived in the western edge of Cannon County on Hollis Creek Road south of the Braxton Community. Many of their ancestors are buried in the McBroom Family Cemetery on a ridge just southwest of the present intersection of Hollis Creek Road and US Highway 70S.

James Allen and Lillie Ann Campbell resided in Cannon County after their marriage, and I have the impression that they were more closely connected to the McBroom family than the Campbell family there. This may have been due to the fact that James Allen's own father, John Watson Campbell, had moved away from Cannon County some time between 1893 and 1900. My grandfather Elam Allen Campbell, the son of James Allen Campbell, kept many contacts with the McBroom relatives in Tennessee and in Texas, and I recall visiting McBroom relatives while visiting in Tennessee with my grandfather in the summer of 1970.

James Allen and Lillie Ann Campbell settled in western Cannon County in a community known as Braxton[75] about four miles west of Woodbury where

---

[74] Sterling Spurlock Brown, *History of Woodbury and Cannon County, Tennessee* (Manchester, Tennessee: Doak Printing Co., 1936), pp. 18 and 23. Nancy Elizabeth McBroom's father was James McBroom (1827-1870), and his father was Alexander McBroom (1798-1888), who was a brother of Henry David McBroom. Some of this family's genealogy is given in Brown, *History of Woodbury and Cannon County*, pp. 207-209.

[75] Tax receipts for James Allen Campbell in Cannon County for 1898 (dated February 17, 1899), 1899 (dated May 5, 1903, *sic*), 1900 (dated January 26, 1901), and 1901 (dated February 18, 1902).

there was a post office between 1889 and 1929, near the intersection of the old Murfreesboro-Woodbury Pike and Locke's Creek Road and just inside Cannon County from the village of Readyville in adjacent Rutherford County. Records kept in our family reveal a few details about the life of James and Lillie Campbell. In June of 1899, for example, James Campbell took out a loan in Woodbury for eleven dollars to purchase a buggy and harness. He repaid the loan by the end of August.[76] Between 1899 and 1900 he supervised the construction of a rock fence for Lillie's uncle W. R. McBroom.[77]

In June, 1900, James Campbell compiled a carefully itemized list (two pages long) of household items purchased "at sale of Mrs. Sullivan's," including a spinning wheel, a churn, irons, various dishes and utensils, and a Seth Thomas clock valued at sixty-five cents.[78] The items purchased also included a wheat crop valued at eight dollars that he harvested and sold to J. R. Hale and Sons of Murfreesboro on July 20, 1900, for $55.[79] He must have carefully calculated that by purchasing, harvesting, and selling the wheat crop he could pay for the items from the household sale. We do not know who the "Mrs. Sullivan" was. According to undocumented family records, Lillie Ann's own mother,

---

[76] Promissory note to Will A. Vick, dated June 17, 1899, and indicated as paid in full on August 29 of the same year.

[77] A receipt and a list of payments (handed down in our family) to workers S. D. Bragg and T. B. Peden, all for dates in the year 1900 although the lists are headed "For 1899-1900."

[78] Itemized list of sale items, handed down in our family.

[79] Receipt from J. R. Hale and Sons to J. A. Campbell dated July 20, 1900.

Nancy (McBroom) Sullivan lived to 1936. I have begun to doubt the veracity of these records, and to suspect that she may indeed have died in 1900.[80]

The first son of James and Lillie, Elam Allen Campbell, had been born on the first of December 1898 in the city of Nashville where James Allen Campbell was working. This indicates that James and Lillie must have been moving back and forth between Nashville and Braxton where they had their permanent residence. A second son, James Thomas or "Jimmie" Campbell, was born in 1900, and a third son, John D. or "Johnny" Campbell, was born in 1904.

### Family of James Allen Campbell (1872-1906)

m. Lillie Ann Sullivan in 1898

Elam Allen Campbell    b. 1898

James T. "Jimmie" Campbell    b. 1900

John D. "Johnny" Campbell    b. 1904

James Allen and Lillie Ann Campbell became associated in Braxton with the Churches of Christ, an American religious movement founded by Scots-Irish Presbyterians Thomas (1763-1854) and Alexander (1788-1866) Campbell, who had become Baptists for a while and then renounced all denominational identification to be known simply as "churches of Christ" or "disciples

---

[80] I have begun to suspect that the family records are incorrect at this point and that Nancy McBroom Sullivan may indeed have died in 1900, in which case this would have been the estate sale for her. The 1900 census shows her son Herman living with Hiram and Maggie Stroud.

of Christ." The "Campbellite" movement had grown from its origins in Pennsylvania and West Virginia and had become prominent through the South and Midwest of the United States in the late 1800s. Elam and Lillie Ann Campbell attended the Braxton Church of Christ in western Cannon County. This church building was destroyed subsequently by a tornado and members of the congregation may have gone to the Sunny Slope Church of Christ on Hollis Creek Road, just south of the site of Braxton. At least, my grandfather Elam Campbell remembered that the family was somehow associated with the Sunny Slope Church of Christ.

Between the births of Jimmie (1900) and Johnny (1904), James Allen, Lillie, Elam, and Jimmie Campbell paid an extended visit to relatives who had settled in Nederland, Texas. Oil had been discovered in Beaumont, not far from Nederland, on January 10, 1901, and during the years 1902 and 1903 there was a strong influx of population into the Beaumont area seeking opportunities related to the discovery of oil. I have reason to believe that Lillie Ann's sister Maggie (Sullivan) Stroud and her husband Hiram Stroud and possibly her brother Herman Sullivan were already living in Nederland at the time when James and Lillie Ann visited there.

A postcard indicates that James Campbell and Lillie Campbell were still in Braxton, Tennessee as late as October 31, 1902.[81] Receipts and other records kept in our family show activities in Texas between January 7, 1903, and May 28 of that year.[82] It would appear that they were at least exploring the possibility of staying in Texas because they paid rent for the months they were there.[83] But they did not remain. A notice in a Nederland newspaper kept in our family (unfortunately without the date for it) observed their departure:

> J. A. Campbell and family left Wednesday for their old home in Murphysboro [sic] Tennessee. We are sorry to loose [sic] these good citizens in this way, but it can not always be our pleasure and selection.[84]

By September 17, 1903, they were back in Braxton, Tennessee. Upon his return, James Campbell had to borrow $30 from a Woodbury attorney, Will A. Vick.[85] This suggests that the Texas trip had exhausted whatever funds the family may have had.

---

[81] A postcard with that date, and also two receipts including a doctor's receipt from McCrary and Son, Physicians, of Woodbury, for that date. I wonder if this means that on 31 October James Allen Campbell went in to Woodbury to pay up debts in advance of his departure for Texas.

[82] Rent receipt from Stearns & Coleman, Port Arthur and Nederland, Texas, dated 7 January 1903; rent receipt from A. Burson, Nederland, dated 7 February, 1903; rent receipt from A. Burson, Nederland, dated 9 March 1903; rent receipt from A. Burson, Nederland, dated 18 April 1903; grocery receipt from King Mercantile Co., Nederland, Texas, dated 28 May, 1903.

[83] See the previous note which refers to rent receipts for January, February, March, and April 1903.

[84] Newspaper clipping preserved in the Campbell family; I have a photocopy from, I believe, the personal effects of Everett A. Campbell.

[85] Promissory note dated 17 September 1903 in Woodbury, Tennessee, securing a loan in the amount of $30.00 for J. A. Campbell from Will A. Vick. Campbell's address is listed as P. O. Box, Braxton, Tennessee.

My grandfather Elam Campbell said that his father James Allen Campbell had worked for a shoe factory in Nashville. Elam himself had been born in Nashville in 1898 and we have receipts from Nashville businesses that show that James Campbell was back working there between February 4, 1905, and December 15th of that year.[86]

Two receipts indicate that James Campbell saw a physician, Dr. Robert L. Hayes, in Nashville on July 19th and July 30th, 1905.[87] This may have been a harbinger of medical problems to come, for he died suddenly of a ruptured appendix on the 6th of July the next year, 1906, at the age of 33. He was buried in the McBroom family cemetery. My grandfather Elam Campbell recalled the difficulty that the wagon carrying his father's coffin had in getting up to the ridge on the day his father was buried.[88]

The life of James Allen Campbell thus ended tragically, and I interpret his life as a quest for a way out

---

[86] Receipt from John O'Hare, Nashville, 4 February 1905 (apparently a rent receipt); rent receipt from John O'Hare, Nashville, 2 May 1905; receipt from Dr. Robert L. Hayes, Nashville, 19 July 1905; receipt from Dr. Robert L. Hayes, Nashville, 30 July 1905; poll tax receipt, Davidson County, Tennessee, 15 December 1905.

[87] An abstract of the *Physicians Record Book 1, 1899-1902* for Nashville, Tennessee, shows a Dr. Robert Lee Hayes who received his medical degree from the University of Tennessee on March 27, 1900, and was given a certificate to practice medicine on April 4 of that year.

[88] My grandfather also recalled that it was snowing on the day of his father's funeral. This leads me to think that the date may have been in January of 1906 rather than June, but all family records I have seen list his death date as July 6. However, these records also list the death date of Lillie Ann Sullivan's father James Sullivan as July 6, 1906, so I suspect that one of the dates is incorrect.

of the rural life that had characterized the Campbells ever since their coming to America and probably before. He wanted to be part of the larger, modern world, but through a series of occupations he did not find a way to do so.

The death of James Allen Campbell was especially tragic for Lillie Ann Campbell who found herself widowed at the age of 32 with three sons, aged 8, 6, and 2, and almost certainly with little or no financial resources. According to family records, her father James Sullivan also died in 1906, and that would have been yet another blow for her and her family.[89] What was she to do?

---

[89] The records at this point are very inconclusive because they give the same date for the death of James Allen Campbell (6 July 1906; see the note above) as for James Sullivan. Moreover, James Sullivan's son Herman is shown as living with Hiram and Maggie Stroud in Cannon County in 1900, and the fact of an estate sale for "Mrs. Sullivan" (see above) leads me to think that both James and Nancy may have died by mid-year 1900.

# CHAPTER 4
# TEXAS

Texas had been part of New Spain and together with Coahuila formed a region of Spanish Mexico. Between 1815 and 1821 Mexico gained its independence from Spain and in the latter year Euro-American people from the United States were given permission to settle in Texas. Texas became an independent republic in 1836, and in 1845, the year John Watson Campbell was born, it became a state of the United States.

By the end of the nineteenth century Texas was beginning to see signs of modernization including the building of railroads across the state.[90] This process was greatly accelerated from 1901 when oil was discovered in great quantity in Texas. It was discovered at a place called Spindletop just south of the city of Beaumont and a few miles north of Nederland on January 10, 1901.[91] It was to this place and its promise of new opportunities that our Campbells were drawn.

## Lillie Ann Campbell in Texas

Many of the Campbell men in the past had made decisions to move their families to a new place to seek a better life where new resources would be available. This time it was Lillie Ann Campbell who made that deci-

---

[90] Cf. John Stricklin Spratt, *The Road to Spindletop: Economic Change in Texas, 1875-1901* (Austin: University of Texas Press, 1955).

[91] This era is described in Paul N. Spellman, *Spindletop Boom Days* (College Station, Texas: Texas A&M University Press, 2001).

sion. She moved with her three sons back to Southeast Texas where she and James and the two older sons had visited before. I do not know exactly when they moved, but it was probably soon after the death of James Allen Campbell, perhaps in 1907.

The 1910 federal census shows her and her three sons living in Nederland, Texas, with her brother Herman Sullivan and Herman's two sons Wiley (age 1) and Raymond (age 4).[92] Her sister Maggie (Sullivan) Stroud is shown in an adjacent enumeration district with her husband Hiram Stroud.[93] In fact, Raymond Sullivan, age 4, is shown in the 1910 census both with the household of Hiram and Maggie Stroud and with his father. Herman Sullivan had been shown in the 1900 census for Cannon County, Tennessee, at age 17 living with Hiram and Maggie Stroud.[94] He had some form of mental illness and ended up in the state hospital in Rusk, Texas, and then later in an institution in Austin, Texas.[95] His sons Raymond and Wiley were raised by Hiram and Maggie Stroud.

Shortly after moving to Texas, Lillie Campbell ran a boarding house at Spindletop, catering to the

---

[92] 1910 census for Jefferson County, Texas, enumeration district 90, p. 53.

[93] 1910 census for Jefferson County, Texas, enumeration district 91, p. 53.

[94] 1900 census for Cannon County, Tennessee, civil district 1, page 5a.

[95] The 1930 census for Cherokee County, Texas, page 15a, enumeration district 2, shows Herman Sullivan as a resident in the Rusk hospital. His grandson Raymond Sullivan, Jr., told me that he visited his grandfather in the Austin institution, and in fact Herman died in Austin in 1952.

workers who had been attracted by the oil rush. Not surprisingly, Lillie's three sons all ended up working in the oil business. The 1920 census shows her with Elam, Johnny, and Jimmie living in the Guffey community near Spindletop and each of the sons is listed as working in the oil fields.[96]

Jimmie, Lillie, and Johnny Campbell, ca. 1915

Lillie Campbell also worked as a quilt maker in her own home. She must have done well enough at her businesses. By 1930 she had purchased a home at 630 Shell Street in the South Park neighborhood of Beau-

---

[96] 1920 census for Jefferson County, Texas, Justice Precinct 6, District 114, p. 9. It is apparent from looking at the lists of people on this page and their occupations that this represents the "boomtown" around Spindletop. Paul N. Spellman's *Spindletop Boom Days* refers to the "Guffey camp" that had grown up near Spindletop in 1901, p. 65.

mont a few miles from the Spindletop oil field and a few blocks from South Park High School.[97] This house was occupied after her death by her son Johnny Campbell and his wife Jack and I knew it well in my childhood. By the time I began to visit the house in the 1950s it had a number of out-buildings, one of which was a chicken shed. The property included a vacant lot next door that was used for a large vegetable garden. Lillie Campbell continued her allegiance to the Churches of Christ after moving to Beaumont, raising her boys in the South Park Church of Christ on Highland Avenue. Hiram and Maggie Stroud also moved to the South Park community to a home on Woodrow Street about five blocks away from Lillie.

By 1930 only Jimmie was shown as living with Lillie Campbell on Shell Street.[98] Elam and Johnny had married sisters from East Texas in 1923 and 1931, respectively, and were pursuing their careers in the oil business.

Lillie Ann Campbell died in 1937 and is buried in the Magnolia Cemetery in Beaumont. By the time of her death she had a number of grandchildren and she had lived to see her three sons live up to their father's ambition to prosper in the modern industrial world. But to give credit where credit is due, it was Lillie Campbell herself who prospered in the modern world after moving to Beaumont. She was a successful businesswoman

---

[97] 1930 census for Jefferson County, Texas, Precinct 6, District 79, p. 13.

[98] Ibid.

and her sons Elam and Johnny would both marry professional women.

### Elam Allen and Verda Odessa (Williams) Campbell

Elam Allen Campbell was the oldest son of James Allen and Lillie Ann Campbell, born on December 1, 1898, in Nashville, Tennessee. The name "Elam" suggests a biblical personal name and the name of an ancient Mesopotamian country (Genesis 10:22 and 14:1; Ezra 4:9) but there was also an English surname "Elam" apparently derived from the village of Elham in Kent. There were persons with the surname Elam in Cannon County, Tennessee, where Elam was born, and at least two persons in the county had Elam as a personal name including John Elam McBroom, a distant cousin of Nancy (McBroom) Sullivan, Elam Campbell's maternal grandmother.[99]

Most of the first nine years of Elam Campbell's life were lived with his family in the Braxton community of Cannon County, Tennessee, though he was born in Nashville and lived there for at least some periods while his father worked there and he had also lived for a few months in Nederland, Texas, when his mother and father visited there. As an older man, he remembered playing in the Tenpenny Cave off Hollis Creek Road in Cannon County, Tennessee.

---

[99] Brown, *History of Woodbury and Cannon County, Tennessee*, pp. 43 (Reuben Elam), 45 (Elam McKnight), and 209 (John Elam McBroom). Census records from the late nineteenth century (1870, 1880, 1900) in Cannon County also show many persons with the surname Elam.

Elam Campbell moved to Texas with his mother and brothers around 1907. They lived in Nederland for a short period then in the community of Guffey near Spindletop where his mother ran a boarding house. He graduated from South Park High School in Beaumont, worked in the oil fields, and ran a filling station with his brother Johnny for a time. He was a very large young man with the build of a football player as photographs show. According to my father, his weight was 280 pounds at one point and friends called him "Big Boy." Later in life Elam managed to lose most of the excess weight. But there was no football playing or other sports for the Campbell boys who were all working to support the family.

Elam Campbell, ca. 1918

Elam Campbell registered for the draft for World War I in 1918 when he was twenty years old, but his status as bread-winner for the family and the fact that oil-field workers were also needed to support the war effort meant that he spent the period of World War I on the home front. His draft registration card shows his occupation at that time as "merchant," with an address in Guffey, Texas.[100]

Five years after the end of World War I and at the beginning of the "roaring twenties," Elam Campbell married Verda Odessa Williams on May 2, 1923. Verda Williams had been born in Buna, Jasper County, Texas, in 1900. She was from a long line of Williamses in Jasper County going back to Stephen Williams (1760-1839), a native of North Carolina who had fought in three wars—the Revolutionary War, the War of 1812, and the Texas Revolution—before becoming one of the pioneer settlers of Jasper County. Verda's father, Edward King Williams, was the great-great-grandson of Stephen Williams. He had worked for the Kirby lumber company and then as foreman for a railroad crew. Verda's mother Annie Eliza Spell was from the Spell family that had settled in the Rosedale community north of Beaumont.[101] At some point in her first ten years of life Verda's parents moved from Buna to the Rosedale

---

[100] Draft registration card for Elam Allen Campbell, dated September 12, 1918.

[101] See Everett Arden Campbell, *Descendants of Benager Spell and Dorethea Foreman* (Privately published; Beaumont, Texas; revised edition of 1991).

community themselves.[102] Verda attended Beaumont High School and then graduated from New South College, a secretarial and training school in Beaumont, on May 20, 1919.[103]

Verda and Elam Campbell, ca. 1925

At the time of her marriage to Elam Campbell in 1923 Verda was serving as secretary to the County Clerk in Hardin County, Texas. She made out her own wedding license and the County Clerk personally paid the fee for it. Later, carrying on the family tradition of brothers marrying sisters, Elam's brother Johnny Campbell would marry Verda's sister Ola Lee "Jack" (or "Jackie") Williams. The two couples were very close,

---

[102] The family appears in the 1900 census for Jasper County, Texas, Precinct 4, District 30, p. 11. They appear in the 1910 census for Jefferson County, Texas, Precinct 1, District 68, p. 38.

[103] Verda Williams' diploma from New South College, in the possession of Ted A. Campbell.

although Jack and Johnny lived in South Park on the south side of Beaumont, and Elam and Verda eventually settled in Rosedale on the far north side of Beaumont.

Although Elam and Johnny Campbell had both grown up in the Churches of Christ, they became Methodists as a result of their marriages to the Williams sisters. Johnny and Jack Campbell attended Roberts Avenue Methodist Church in Beaumont. After moving to the Rosedale community, Elam and Verda would join the Rosedale Methodist Church that later became St. Luke's United Methodist Church in Beaumont. Elam served as treasurer of the congregation for many years and Verda produced its newsletter.

Elam Campbell worked for the Yount-Lee Oil Company of Beaumont, a company that had been formed by Miles Franklin ("Frank") Yount in 1914 with the financial backing of Thomas Peter Lee of Houston. The company specialized in drilling deeper wells than had been drilled in the past in oil fields that had been considered depleted. Elam Campbell knew Frank Yount personally and my father has in his possession a set of tools that Mr. Yount gave my grandfather one year at Christmas. Elam became a driller and would eventually become a field foreman and then a field supervisor for the company. The company was sold in the 1930s to Stanolin Oil (Standard Oil of Indiana) and eventually became part of Amoco. Elam Campbell worked for the company through its various changes. His work involved not only traveling by himself, but some relocations for the family early on in his career. He covered a number of oil fields in Southeast Texas including Anahuac, Liberty, Hull-Daisetta, and West Beaumont. According to my father, traveling salesmen would ply him with candy while he was on the job, and this didn't help to keep his weight in check.

Elam Campbell came to be known for his skill in drilling wells and he also utilized these skills to drill water wells. He built a drilling rig from a Model A Ford and drilled wells for families in the Rosedale community where he and Verda settled.

At some point in the mid to late 1920s Elam and Verda Campbell had a home built at 6135 Garner Road in the Rosedale community.[104] The home was designed and built by Sid Stern of Beaumont and it cost them about $3,500. The land for the home was sold to them by Verda's father Edward King Williams who had also settled on Garner Road. The home originally had an outhouse but the city supplied water connections shortly after they moved in and a bathroom was added. Elam continued to travel and the family would be away for months or a year (for example, they spent several months in High Island, Texas), but they kept the house while they were away, renting it out during longer stays. The Rosedale community was at that time an outlying suburb of Beaumont where families could have large lots. Verda and Elam had more than two acres

---

[104] The family is shown living on Garner Road in the 1930 census for Jefferson County, Texas, Precinct 1, District 45, p. 105. The address 6135 was not assigned until some time later, perhaps when Rosedale was incorporated into Beaumont.

with a barn and they raised vegetables and kept chickens, horses, and milk cows on the property.

The oldest son of Verda and Elam Campbell, Everett Arden Campbell, had been born while they were living in Vinton, Louisiana, in 1924. Their son Gene Allen Campbell and their daughter Maggie Marie Campbell were born in Beaumont in 1926 and 1930, respectively. The children attended the Voth-Rosedale Elementary School (now Roy H. Guess Elementary School in Beaumont) and then went on to Beaumont High School.

**Family of Elam Allen Campbell (1898-1995)**

m. Verda Odessa Williams in 1923

Everett Arden Campbell b. 1924

Gene Allen Campbell b. 1926

Maggie Marie Campbell b. 1930

After the births and upbringing of her children, Verda Campbell resumed her professional career as a secretary. She served for many years as the secretary for the Wayne Brown Insurance Agency of Beaumont, working in the downtown Beaumont office of that agency where she could eat at the Piccadilly Cafeteria nearby.

Everett and Gene Campbell both served in the United States Navy in World War II. According to my father, Gene Campbell, Everett enlisted in the Navy on Pearl Harbor Day, Sunday December 7, 1941. Apparently enlistment centers were actually opened on that day. Within four or five weeks, Everett shipped out on the heavy cruiser *USS Portland*. He served in the Pacific as a gunner's mate on that ship and toward the end of the war he was sent to Columbia, South Carolina, for officer's training.

Gene Campbell remained in high school through the spring semester 1942 and enlisted in the Navy in the summer of that year with Beaumont friends Gordon Earl Cole and Joe McCann. He shipped out to the Pacific from Union Lake, Seattle, Washington, and served on *LST 461*. LST denoted "Landing Ship Tank," a vessel more then three hundred feet long designed to carry tanks and other motorized vehicles for amphibious assault landings. The LST was popularly dubbed "Large Slow Target." At the end of the war Gene Campbell was assigned to the *USS Gillis*, a ship involved in survey work around Bikini Atoll where atomic bombs were being tested. He was offered the possibility of remaining for two additional weeks to witness a detonation and was even offered an advancement in rank for doing so, but he elected to return home. His transport came into the US port of Astoria, Oregon. From there he went inland to Portland, and the next morning he found himself shaving next to his friend Gordon Earl Cole whom he had not seen for the two years they were in the Navy.

After the war Everett Campbell became a blacksmith employed by the Mobil Refinery in Beaumont. He married Lucy Hugus in 1946 and their son King Allen Campbell was born in 1947. King was the first grandchild of Elam and Verda Campbell. Everett and Lucy and King lived in the north end of Beaumont through the years when King was in high School. King attended

French High School and the family belonged to Asbury United Methodist Church in Beaumont.

Gene Allen Campbell and his sister Maggie Marie Campbell both married into the Cammack family that also lived on Garner Road and were fellow members of the Rosedale Methodist Church. Gene Campbell married Autie Lucretia Cammack in 1946. He became an electrical instrument technician employed by the Goodyear Beaumont Chemical Plant. He and Lucretia Campbell had four sons: Warren Gene (born in 1948), Ted Allen (born in 1953), Mark Elam, (born in 1956), and Glen Ed (born in 1961). They lived for many years at 3185 Gilbert Street in Beaumont then moved in the summer of 1969 into a home at 545 Potter Drive built by Gene Campbell himself with help from his father Elam, his uncle Johnny, and others. The family was active at Memorial United Methodist Church in Beaumont until the late 1970s when Gene and Lucretia joined the congregation of Cathedral in the Pines Christian Center.

Maggie Marie Campbell married Lester Eugene Cammack (Sr.) in 1952 and they settled into a home on Lawrence Drive in a Beaumont suburb north of Rosedale in the 1950s. They would live there through the 1980s. Eugene worked as a salesman at Oil City Tractors in Beaumont. Their children were Elizabeth Ann ("Beth," born in 1953), Lester Eugene, Jr. ("Gene," born in 1955), Marilyn Marie (born in 1958), James Elam ("Jim," born in 1961), and a baby Carolyn Sue who was born in May of 1963 and died tragically of an acute illness eight months later. Their family was very active at St. Luke's United Methodist Church.

During the late 1950s and the early 1960s the Campbell family was thriving in Beaumont. Children and grandchildren were regularly at their home on Garner Road on Sunday afternoons, holidays, and many other occasions as well, and grandchildren regularly spent weeks in the summer with Elam and Verda Campbell on Garner Road. My mother and brothers and I and a number of cousins as well spent the night of June 27, 1957, on palettes on the floor of their house while hurricane Audrey struck Beaumont. We were also frequently together at the home of Johnny and Jack Campbell in South Park.

Grandsons Mark, Glen (seated) and Ted Campbell
with Elam Campbell at the Readyville Mill
in Tennessee in the summer of 1970

Elam and Verda Campbell loved to travel by car, and after Elam retired in the 1970s they joined a traveling group that toured the country with travel trailers. Elam particularly loved returning to Cannon County, Tennessee. He taught us as children with a wink of the eye that the capital of Tennessee was Woodbury. An unsubstantiated rumor in our family has that one of my brothers actually blurted this out in response to a teacher's question, "What is the capital of Tennessee?"

Verda and Elam Campbell's first great grandchild Kelly Ann Campbell was born in 1975 and by 1992 there were eighteen great grandchildren. They are the tenth generation after Malcolm and Isabella Campbell.

Verda Campbell lived to see some but not all of her great grandchildren before she died on April 15, 1983, after a lengthy illness. Two months later, on June 14th, Elam Campbell made out his final will, witnessed by C. Scott Mann, Jr., and Chilton O'Brien.[105] In the early 1990s the house at 6135 Garner Road was sold and Elam moved into a smaller and more modern home built by Everett Campbell on the same road. He continued to go for walks in the evening and to write daily in his diary. Elam Campbell lived there until his death on July 21, 1995, just three years and a few months shy of being a hundred years old.

Elam and Verda Campbell are buried at the Forest Lawn cemetery on the banks of the Neches River in Beaumont along with their daughter Maggie Marie and grand-daughter Carolyn Sue Cammack. Forest Lawn

---

[105] Will of Elam Allen Campbell signed June 14, 1983. I do not know if there had been an earlier will, but this was the will that was probated.

cemetery is adjacent to the Magnolia Cemetery where Elam's brother Johnny and Verda's sister Jack are buried, and where Johnny and Elam's mother Lillie Ann Campbell also rests.

**A Campbell Journey into the Twenty-First Century**

Maggie Marie (Campbell) Cammack died in November of 2000 and her brother Everett Campbell died in 2002. Everett's wife Lucy (Hugus) Campbell died in May of 2003.

In the year 2004 a new generation began appearing with the birth of Maggie Marie's great granddaughter Britney Danyell Murrell, followed by Bradley Lyons in 2006, Madelyn Paige Campbell and Peter Allen Wilbanks in 2008, then David Allen Grosso and Peyton Cooper Murrell in 2009. This new generation is the eleventh generation after our immigrant ancestor Malcolm and his wife Isabella (Huston) Campbell. Two of the baby boys of this new generation have the middle name "Allen," a middle name carried through seven generations since the time of Thomas Campbell and his friend Allen Morgan in Tennessee.

# Conclusion

The Campbell journey narrated in this book extends from the 1740s when Malcolm and Isabella Campbell came to Virginia to the present time. It covers eleven generations including Malcolm and Isabella, twelve if we include his father Archibald, though the historical evidence for his father is not as strong as the evidence for Malcolm himself. It is a story that proceeds from Scotland probably by way of Ireland to colonial Pennsylvania and Virginia then to Tennessee and Texas. It tells the story of a family that began as Scottish Presbyterians who became Baptists and then adherents of the Churches of Christ in Tennessee and then became Methodists in Texas.

This is a story of a family with a desire to keep moving to find new opportunities. Malcolm Campbell was one of the first settlers on the Great Lick as the Shenandoah Valley was opening up to settlement by Scots-Irish people. His son William Campbell made a provision in his will that his sons could find land "in the Western Country" to settle. William's son Archibald Campbell came to Wilson County, Tennessee, within five years of the opening of that area to Euro-American settlers. Archibald's great grandson James Allen Campbell showed up in Southeast Texas within 36 months of the discovery of oil at Spindletop and although he did not stay, his wife Lillie Ann (Sullivan) Campbell returned there with her three boys. In the whole narrative of seven Campbell men listed in the introduction, only one remained in the county in which he was born. That was William Campbell, but William Campbell himself recognized that his sons would want to move on westward. His father Malcolm Campbell moved from Ireland to Virginia; his son Archibald moved from Virginia to Tennessee. Archibald's son Thomas Campbell moved from Wilson County to Cannon County. Thomas's son John Watson Campbell moved from Cannon County to Warren County to Lawrence County to Maury County where he died. John Watson's son James Allen Campbell lived for most of his life in Cannon County but had lived in Warren County (Dibrell), Davidson County (Nashville), and in Jefferson County, Texas (Nederland), for particular periods. James Allen's son Elam Campbell was born in Cannon County, Tennessee, and moved to Jefferson County, Texas, as a child. This is the story of a family with "itchy feet."

Archibald Campbell (ca. 1770-ca. 1871) is the real link in this genealogical chain. He was born in the area where our immigrant ancestor Malcolm Campbell settled and he died in the county where my grandfather Elam Campbell was born. I still want to know more about him. His complex itinerary of travels contributes to the difficulty in tracking him from Virginia to Wilson County, Tennessee, and then to Cannon County, Tennessee. He is fairly well documented in the public records of Wilson County, Tennessee, as an early settler there but he is not remembered in histories of the region, perhaps because his descendants did not remain in that county. His father was slaveholder and he was not. One of his sons (Archibald Campbell, Jr.) moved from Tennessee to Illinois in the very decade in which the Civil War occurred. One of his grandsons named his dog "Old Forrest" for the founder of the Ku Klux Klan. I suppose that was meant as a compliment, but I would like to know more about him and his family.

I would also like to know more about Malcolm Campbell: where he came from in Ireland or Scotland, and about his ancestors. The development of more extensive samples of DNA in the future may enable us to know more about our longer history.

But for now, this is the story of our Campbell journey as I have begun to put it together. The Duke of Argyll states in his greeting in this book that we have to be impressed by the dedication and determination of our ancestors. We do indeed. We honor their memories as we look to the future with our own families and our Campbell journey moves forward. *Ne obliviscaris*: do not forget.

# Genealogical Information

Generation 1: **Malcolm Campbell**
b. ca. 1715 in Northern Ireland (Ulster) or Scotland
d. 1763 in Augusta County, colonial Virginia
m. **Isabella Huston** (Houston)

    **Archibald Campbell** (the Elder)
    b. 1743 in Augusta County, colonial Virginia
    d. 1774 in Botetourt County, colonial Virginia

    **Elizabeth Campbell**
    b. 1747 in Augusta County, colonial Virginia
    m. **William Simpson**

        **John Simpson**
        (birth and death dates unknown)

        **Archibald Simpson**
        (birth and death dates unknown)

    **Mary Campbell**
    b. 1749 in Augusta County, colonial Virginia

    **William Campbell** [continues below]

    **Rebecca Campbell**
    b. 1751 in Augusta County, colonial Virginia

    **Jane (Jean) Campbell**
    b. 1754 in Augusta County, colonial Virginia
    m. **Nathaniel Evans**
        b. ca. 1750

Generation 2: **William Campbell** (the Elder)
b. ca. 1750 in Augusta County, colonial Virginia
d. 1804 in Botetourt County, Virginia
m. Elizabeth McDonald (?)

    **Thomas Campbell**
    b. ca. 1770 in Augusta or Botetourt County, Virginia

    **Archibald Campbell** [continues below]

    **John Campbell**
    b. ca. 1777 in Botetourt County, Virginia
    m. Rebecca

        **Robert Campbell**
        b. 1804, d. 1881

        **Susanna Campbell**
        b. 1808, d. 1884

        **Clack R. Campbell**
        b. 1809, d. 1881

        **Matilda Campbell**
        b. 1814, d. 1888

m. **Susannah Dabney**
m. in 1781

    **William Campbell** ("Jr.")
    b. ca. 1781 in Botetourt County, Virginia
    m. **Frances Seaton**
        b. 1782

        **Margaret Tamzey Campbell**
        b. 1817, d. 1887

    Martha Ann Campbell
    b. 1820

    Seaton Campbell
    b. 1823, d. 1908

    Alphenia Campbell
    b. 1825

    Chapman Campbell
    b. 1829

James Campbell
b. ca. 1783 in Botetourt County, Virginia

Rhoda "Rhody" Campbell
b. ca. 1784 in Botetourt County, Virginia
d. 1860 in Wilson County, Tennessee
m. **Elisha Winters** in 1819 in Wilson County, Tennessee
m. **Ambrose Holland** in 1822 in Wilson Co., Tennessee
m. **James Cropper** in 1824 in Wilson County, Tennessee

    Lovina Cropper
    b. 1802, d. 1860

    Hiram S. Cropper
    b. 1822

Polly Campbell
b. ca. 1786 in Botetourt County, Virginia
m. **Simon Camper** in 1810 in Botetourt County, Virginia

Generation 3: **Archibald "Arch" Campbell** (the Younger, Sr.)
b. ca. 1770 in Augusta County, colonial Virginia[106]
d. ca. 1871 in Cannon County, Tennessee
m. **Rebecca Jacobs**
    b. December 15, 1784
    d. between 1854 and 1860

**Edward Gaston Campbell**
b. September 16, 1806, in Wilson County, Tennessee
d. March 18, 1895
m. **Arsenath C. Maxwell**
    b. 1808 in Ohio
    d. before 1880
m. on December 21, 1827, in Wilson County, Tennessee
m. **Esther L. Vaught** (b. 1813) in 1880

**Thomas Campbell** [continues below]

**Archibald ("Archabald") Campbell, Jr.**
b. ca. 1815 in Wilson County, Tennessee
m. **Mary Ann Gaither** in 1842
Family moved to Illinois in early 1860s

**Amos Campbell**
b. ca. 1815 in Wilson County, Tennessee
m. **Nancy Belt** in 1842
m. **Esther Williams** 1850
m. **Laurena Davenport** in 1868
m. **Anna J. Vaught** in 1875

---

[106] His birth was in Botetourt County if it was in 1772 or after, since Botetourt County was formed from Augusta County in 1772.

Generation 4: **Thomas Campbell**
b. June, 1807, in Round Lick, Wilson County, Tennessee
d. March 6, 1886, in Cannon County, Tennessee
m. **Anna Gaither**
    b. 1822 in North Carolina
    d. September 18, 1849, in Cannon County, Tennessee
m. on January 21, 1840, in Cannon County, Tennessee

    **Mahala ("Mahaly" or "Haly") Campbell**
    b. December 10, 1840 in Cannon County, Tennessee
    d. May 20, 1914 in Cannon County, Tennessee
    m. **John Greer Armstrong**
        b. 1838
        d. August 25, 1865
    m. in 1860 in Cannon County, Tennessee

        **Thomas Knox Armstrong**
        b. June 10, 1858 in Cannon County, Tennessee
        d. February 25, 1940, in Cannon County, Tennessee

        **Clinton Armstrong**
        b. 1860 in Cannon County, Tennessee

        **Sam Armstrong**
        b. January 27, 1860 in Cannon County, Tennessee
        d. May 19, 1909 in Cannon County, Tennessee

        **Mary Clista Armstrong**
        b. December 31, 1861, in Cannon County, Tennessee
        d. May 11, 1903, in Cannon County, Tennessee

Mary Ann Campbell
b. June 29, 1842, in Cannon County, Tennessee
d. February 26, 1926, Cannon Co., Tennessee
m. John Pittard Dobbs
    b. June 1, 1837, in Shawnee, Gallatin County, Illinois;
    d. May 2, 1910, in Cannon County, Tennessee
m. on May 12, 1867

    Ann S. Dobbs
    b. March 1, 1867, in Cannon County, Tennessee
    d. September, 1944, in Cannon County, Tennessee

    Thomas E. Dobbs
    b. October 20, 1869 in Cannon County, Tennessee
    d. June, 1870, in Canon County, Tennessee

    James "Jim" Dobbs
    b. May 28, 1871 in Cannon County, Tennessee
    d. November 10, 1896, in Cannon County, Tennessee

    Colista Angeline Dobbs
    b. March 20, 1874, in Cannon County, Tennessee
    d. February 26, 1954

    Alta P. Dobbs
    b. March 18, 1875, in Cannon County, Tennessee
    d. April 16, 1946, in Cannon County, Tennessee

    John P. Dobbs
    b. November, 1878, in Cannon County, Tennessee
    d. January 29, 1954, in Nashville, Tennessee

    Pernisia Dobbs
    b. January 1879, in Cannon County, Tennessee

**Terah Jane Dobbs**
b. July 4, 1881, in Cannon County, Tennessee
d. February 2, 1981, in Cannon County, Tennessee

**Jesse Howell Dobbs**
b. October 30, 1886, in Cannon County, Tennessee
d. April 27, 1964, in Madison, Tennessee

John Watson Campbell [continues below]

**Amos Dison Campbell**
b. January 2, 1847, in Cannon County, Tennessee
d. April 12, 1911, in Cannon County, Tennessee
m. **Serena Morgan**
    b. March 25, 1846, in Cannon County, Tennessee
    d. January 2, 1914, in Cannon County, Tennessee
m. on October 22, 1868, in Cannon County, Tennessee

    **John Robert Campbell**
    b. May 11, 1870, in Cannon County, Tennessee
    d. March 13, 1906, in Cannon County, Tennessee

    **Thomas Allen Campbell**
    b. June 22, 1872, in Cannon County, Tennessee

    **George Lee Campbell**
    b. December 27, 1873, in Cannon County, Tennessee

    **Jesse Dison Campbell**
    b. October 4, 1875, in Cannon County, Tennessee
    d. December 6, 1945, in Cannon County, Tennessee

    **Lou Ann Campbell**
    b. June 5, 1878, in Cannon County, Tennessee
    d. February 16, 1962, in Cannon County, Tennessee

    **James Edward Campbell**
    b. February 12, 1880, in Woodbury, Tennessee
    d. October 12, 1918, in Los Angeles, California

    **Sephythia Isabell Campbell**
    b. 1882, in Cannon County, Tennessee
    d. April 18, 1953, in Cannon County, Tennessee
    m. **Elvie Hatten Reed** (1879-1952)
    m. in 1912 in Cannon County, Tennessee

    **Ada Inez Campbell**
    b. February 29, 1884, in Cannon County, Tennessee
    d. February 9, 1974, in Lakeland, Polk County, Florida


  **Buson Campbell**
  b. 1848 (died as infant)

m. **Pernetia (Witherspoon) Armstrong** in 1851

Generation 5: **John Watson Campbell**
b. April 30, 1845 in Cannon County, Tennessee
d. January 31, 1915, in Maury County, Tennessee
m. **Serecia Emalina ("Reca" or "Reacy") Morgan**
    b. February 13, 1845
    d. June 1893
m. on January 31, 1867, in Cannon County, Tennessee

    **Rosannah A. Campbell**
    b. January 22, 1868 in Cannon County, Tennessee
    d. July 24, 1879

    **Albert L. Campbell**
    b. August 10, 1870
    m. **Martha Arnett** on 1 November, 1895

    Omer Campbell
    b. 1897

    Chester Campbell
    b. 1898

James Allen Campbell [continues below]

Mary Ann Campbell
b. July 29, 1875

Serena Callie Campbell
b. July 27, 1877
m. John Thurston

    J. Lawrence Thurston

Lydia J. "Liddy" Campbell
b. April 2, 1880
d. October 6, 1903

Edward Dison Campbell
b. May 10, 1882
d. November 25, 1926
m. Elizabeth Moss
    b. August 11, 1880
    d. April 26, 1930

    John William Campbell
    b. July 9, 1902 , in Tennessee

    Carnell Tracy Campbell
    b. February 18, 1904, in Tennessee

    James M. Campbell
    b. December 3, 1905, in Tennessee

>> Ila Okla Campbell
>> b. March 20, 1908, in Tennessee

>> Coland Edward Campbell
>> b. September 19, 1910, in Tennessee
>> d. December 12, 1911, in Tennessee

>> Walter Erwin Campbell
>> b. December 31, 1912, in Tennessee

>> Ada Lois Campbell
>> b. May 1, 1917, in Tennessee

>> Lorelle Campbell
>> b. March 12, 1915, in Tennessee

>> Alexander Campbell
>> b. November 7, 1919, in Tennessee

>> Leona Campbell
>> b. June 9, 1925, in Tennessee

Nettie A. Campbell
b. March 30, 1885

Morgan Thomas Campbell
b. November 6, 1887
d. May 24, 1977
m. Myrtle

> Elizabeth Campbell
> b. about 1913

Carl Campbell
b. about 1916

m. **Virginia Cothran Fuller** in 1971

Generation 6: **James Allen Campbell**
b. September 21, 1872, in Cannon County, Tennessee
d. July 6, 1906, in Cannon County, Tennessee
m. **Lillie Ann Sullivan**
b. August 2, 1874, in Cannon County, Tennessee
d. March 16, 1935, in Beaumont, Jefferson County, Texas
m. on 23 June 1898

**Elam Allen Campbell** [continues below]

**James Thomas "Jimmie" Campbell**
b. October 8, 1900 in Cannon County, Tennessee
m. **Myrtle Ellen Spugs**

**James Thomas Campbell**
b. February 26, 1932, in Caldwell, Texas

**Hiram Kirk Campbell**
b. June 4, 1933, in Caldwell, Texas

**Billy Marion Campbell**
b. April 17, 1936, in Caldwell, Texas

**John "Johnny" Campbell**
b. July 4, 1904, in Cannon County, Tennessee
d. September 1976 in Beaumont, Jefferson County, Texas
m. **Ola Lee "Jack" (or "Jackie") Williams**
b. September 19, 1906, in Buna, Jasper County, Texas
d. December 4, 1991, in Beaumont, Texas
m. on May 21, 1931 in Calcasieu Parish, Louisiana

John Hubert Campbell
b. June 2, 1938 in Beaumont, Jefferson County, Texas
m. **Martha Blanche Sanders**
m. on December 22, 1959 in Beaumont, Texas

Sally Laverne Campbell
b. August 27, 1940 in Houston, Harris County, Texas
d. August 26, 1982, in Beaumont, Jefferson Co., Texas
m. **Eugene Wheat** on June 13, 1964

Generation 7: **Elam Allen Campbell**
b. December 1, 1898, in Nashville, Davidson Co., Tennessee
d. July 21, 1995, in Beaumont, Jefferson County, Texas
m. **Verda Odessa Williams**
    b. April 28, 1900, in Buna, Jasper County, Texas
    d. April 15, 1983, in Beaumont, Jefferson County, Texas
m. on May 2, 1923, in Hardin County, Texas

Everett Arden Campbell
b. February 2, 1924, in Vinton, Calcasieu Par., Louisiana
d. February 22, 2002, in Beaumont, Jefferson Co., Texas
m. **Mary Louise "Lucy" Hugus**
    b. September 5, 1919
    d. March 2, 2003, in Bullard, Smith County, Texas
m. on 28 December, 1946.

King Allen Campbell
b. November 27, 1947 in Beaumont, Texas
m. **Kathryn Ann Blalock**
m. January 26, 1973, in Beaumont, Texas

Kelly Ann Campbell
b. June 27, 1975
d. December 4, 1997, in Austin, Texas

m. Angela Anderson Forman
m. April 3, 1982

**Gene Allen Campbell**
b. November 22, 1926, in Beaumont, Texas
   (birth certificate shows November 11, 1926)
m. **Autie Lucretia Cammack**
   b. February 23, 1926 in Beaumont, Texas
m. on December 22, 1946, in Beaumont, Texas

   **Warren Gene Campbell**
   b. June 26, 1948, in Beaumont, Jefferson County, Texas

   m. **Sally Ann Sauls**
   m. on March 27, 1969 in Falls Church, Virginia
   m. **Stephanie Sue Hand**
      b. November 5, 1950
   m. on August 16, 1980, in Houston, Harris Co., Texas

      **Stephanie Alexandra Campbell**
      b. November 16, 1985, in Houston, Texas

   m. **Patricia Jean "Pat" (Sandusky) Esslinger**
      b. February 25, 1949
   m. on April 11, 2005

      **Kelly Esslinger**
      (daughter of Pat by previous marriage)
      b. 1977

   **Ted Allen Campbell**
   b. September 3, 1953, in Beaumont, Texas
   m. **Dale Marie Fick**
      b. February 6, 1954
   m. June 7, 1975, in Houston, Harris County, Texas

Elizabeth Marie Campbell
b. May 14, 1983, in Dallas, Dallas County, Texas

Lydia Anne Campbell
b. September 25, 1986, in Durham, North Carolina

**Mark Elam Campbell**
b. September 21, 1956, in Beaumont, Texas
m. **Toni Ann McGowan**
b. October 19, 1958
m. on December 31, 1977

Cheryl Lynn Campbell
b. July 22, 1978
m. Richard R. Foss II
m. on December 27, 1996 in Jasper, Texas
m. David Michael Grosso
b. October 20, 1977 in Plantation, Florida
m. on November 24, 2001, in Pensacola, Florida

David Allen Grosso
b. February 17, 2009, in Fort Worth, Texas

Allan Gene Campbell
b. April 21, 1980
m. Jeannie Shannon Mood
b. October 20, 1978
m. on June 4, 2005, in New Orleans, Louisiana

Madelyn Paige Campbell
b. February 17, 2008, in Eureka, California

m. **Marion Nell Miller**
b. August 2, 1957
m. on September 27, 1985 in Beaumont, Texas

Jason Plumley
(son of Marion by previous marriage)
b. August 3, 1981
m. **Rachel Lyons**
    b. September 5, 1981
m. on August 28, 2009, in Virginia Beach, Virginia

    Bradley Lyons
    (son of Rachel by previous marriage)
    b. November 25, 2006

Allison Michelle Campbell
b. January 20, 1987 Ellis County, Texas
m. **Matthew Reid Barrett**
m. December 20, 2009 [anticipated]

Wesley Taylor Campbell
b. August 15, 1992 in Jasper, Texas

**Glen Ed Campbell**
b. January 9, 1961, in Beaumont, Jefferson Co., Texas
m. **Anita Rieck**
    b. February 6, 1959
m. on October 1, 1988, in Austin, Travis County, Texas

    Elam Lawrence Campbell
    b. April 18, 1991, in Austin, Travis County, Texas

**Maggie Marie Campbell**
b. September 20, 1930, in Beaumont, Jefferson Co., Texas
d. November 29, 2000, in Port Neches, Texas
m. **Lester Eugene Cammack**
    b. September 20, 1930
m. on January 6, 1952 in Beaumont, Jefferson Co., Texas

Elizabeth Ann "Beth" Cammack
b. January 8, 1953, in Beaumont, Jefferson Co., Texas
m. **Gerald Charles "Gerry" Wilbanks**
    b. February 3, 1953
m. on April 16, 1973, in Beaumont, Texas

    Susan Lyn Wilbanks
    b. May 1, 1978
    m. **Randal Dewayne Murrell**

        Britney Danyell Murrell
        b. May 4, 2004

        Peyton Cooper Murrell
        b. July 9, 2009

    Coby Lee Wilbanks
    b. May 2, 1981
    m. Samantha Cooper

    Luke Patrick Wilbanks
    b. December 1, 1982, in Beaumont, Texas
    m. **Elizabeth Ann "Betsy" Hipps**
        b. January 31, 1981, in Memphis, Tennessee
    m. December 11, 2004, in Diboll, Texas

        Peter Allen Wilbanks
        b. July 9, 2008, in Dallas, Texas

Lester Eugene "Gene" Cammack, Jr.
b. January 31, 1955, in Beaumont, Jefferson Co., Texas
m. **Sharon Sue Dixon**
    b. June 15, 1957
m. on June 4, 1977, in Beaumont, Jefferson Co., Texas

> **Matthew Eugene Cammack**
> b. June 5, 1979, in Amarillo, Texas
>
> **Adam Cecil Cammack**
> b. July 23, 1983, in Beaumont, Texas

**Marilyn Marie Cammack**
b. December 3, 1958, in Beaumont, Texas
m. **Gary Wayne Myers**
> b. December 10, 1954
m. on May 10, 1980

> **Jamie Marie Myers**
> b. November 29, 1982 in Beaumont, Texas
>
> **Christopher Gary Myers**
> b. August 6, 1986, in Beaumont, Texas

**James Elam "Jim" Cammack**
b. May 15, 1961, in Beaumont, Jefferson County, Texas
m. **Nancy Orchid McCollum**
> b. October 13, 1956
m. on January 7, 1989

> **Alexander James Cammack**
> b. April 21, 1992, in Beaumont, Texas

**Carolyn Sue Cammack**
b. May 12, 1963, in Beaumont, Jefferson County, Texas
d. February 7, 1964, in Beaumont, Jefferson Co., Texas

# HISTORICAL DOCUMENTS

\*\*\* denotes illegible text

## Item 1. 1761 Summary of the Will of Malcolm Campbell

"His will made in February, 1761, and proved in June, 1763, provided that his wife, Isabella, should have one third of his personal estate and a living from the place; son, Archibald, to have 200 acres off the upper end of the plantation adjoining the Long Lick and a survey on Mill Creek; William to have the other half of the plantation containing all the houses and improvements; the two sons, Archibald and William, and four daughters, Elizabeth, Mary, Jane and Rebecca together to have the rest of the movable estate; Samuel Lyle and son Archibald to be executors."

**Source**: Augusta County, Virginia, Will Book 3, page 266; summarized in Kegley, Virginia Frontier, p. 333. Witnesses to the will were Archibald Alexander, Daniel Lyle, and Nathan Peoples.

## Item 2. 1774 Will of Archibald Campbell ("the Elder")

I give and bequeath in the manner following: It is my desire that my just debts be paid. My Estate by my Executor, hereafter named. I give and bequeath to my brother William Campbell's oldest son Thomas Campbell my plantation whereon I now live. I give and bequeath to my brother William Campbell one tract of land in Pittsylvania laying on Tomahawk Creek. Also all my wearing clothes. I also give and bequeath unto William Simpson's son, John Simpson one plantation laying in Botetourt County on Mill Creek that was willed to me by my father. I also give to William Simpson's son, Archibald Simpson one tract of land enjoining the aforesaid tract on the lower side of Mill Creek.

I also give to my sister, Jean Campbell one negro girl named Pegg about nine years of age. In case my sister, Jean does not intermarry with Nathaniel Evans, brother of Peter Evans But if my sister Jean should marry the said Evans, it is my will that the Negro girl Pegg shall be sold and the money from the sale to be equally divided between my brother William's son Thomas Campbell & William Simpson's sons, John and Archibald Simpson.

My will and desire is that all my movable estate be appraised and sold and the money used to pay my debts and if any is left over, it is to be equally divided between William Simpson's sons, John and Archibald Simpson

I appoint my brother, William Campbell executor of this my last will and testament. This 8th day of January 1774. Witnesses: John Bowman, James Ritchie, James McNeele (McNeill)

Source: Botetourt County, Virginia, Will Book A, p. 78. This will was probated in Botetourt County, Virginia, on April 17th 1774. Transcription from internet sources.

### Item 3. 1799 Will of William Campbell

In the name of God Amen I William Campbell of Botetourt County being sick & weak of Body, but in perfect Senses & memory of mind do make ordain constitute & appoint this my last will and Testament in the manner & form following (viz) First I give my soul to Almighty God hoping and trusting in Jesus Christ for life & Justification Secondly I give my Body to the Earth from whence it was taken to be buried in a desent [sic] manner without pomp or vanity according to the discretion of my Executor hereinafter mentioned and as for my worldly Estate which it hath pleased God to bless me with I give & dispose of as followeth

Item: I give to my Son Thomas Campbell Forty Pounds. Item I give to my Son Archibald Campbell Forty Pounds likewise two Hundred Acres Land in the Western Country's which is to be hereafter purchased by my Executor

Item I give to my Son William Campbell four Hundred Acres Land in the Western Country's which is to be purchased hereafter by my Executors likewise one Negro Boy named Daniel when he comes to the age of twenty years likewise one good Horse Saddle & Bridle and one Bay filly three years old

Item I give to my Son James Campbell four Hundred Acres of Land to be purchased hereafter by my Executors in the Western Country likewise one Horse Saddle & Bridle & one Negro to be equal in value as the above mentioned Daniel to be Rec'd when he comes to the age of twenty years

Item I give to my Son John Campbell Four Hundred Acres Land in the Western Country which is to be purchased hereafter by my Executors likewise one Horse Saddle & Bridle and one Negro to be equal in value as the within named Daniel

Item I give to my Daughter Rhoda Campbell forty five Pounds in cash and one Horse Saddle & Bridle when she comes to the Age of Eighteen Years

Item I give to my Daughter Polly Campbell forty five Pounds in cash and one Horse Saddle & Bridle when she comes to the Age of Eighteen Years

Item I give to my loving wife Susannah all my household Furniture & Six of the best Cows and Calves in my Stock and my [***] mare and colt and the two horses named by the name of Streamer and Warner during her life, and after her death to be divided Between my five children (viz) William, James, John, Rhoda, and Polly, likewise my desire is that my two Mares [***] be sold and all my Lands and part of my Stock of Hogs & the money arising from such sale after my Just Debts be paid to be apply'd to the Purchasing of the within mentioned Land & Negroes likewise my desire is that my wife Susannah keep my two Negroes Dingo and Amey during her life and further my desire is that my loving wife live on the tract of land that is to be hereafter purchased for my Son John during life or widowhood

And lastly I nominate and appoint loving wife Susannah and Matthew Pate Executrix and Executor of this my last will and Testament in witness whereof I have hereunto set my hand and seal this 4th day of June 1799

Signed and acknowledged }
in presence of                Wm Campbell {seal}
Stephen Ferrall
Elizabeth (x) Jarrett
Hannah (x) Manicle

At Botetourt April Court 1804

This Instrument of writing purporting to be the last Will & Testament of William Campbell dec'd was Exhibited in Court and proven by the oath of Stephen Ferrell & Elizabeth Jarrett Witnesses thereto & ordered to be Recorded

**Source**: Botetourt County, Virginia, Will Book B, pp. 56-57. Transcribed by Ted A. Campbell from photocopy.

## Item 4. 1854 Deed of Archibald Campbell (Sr.) to Archibald Campbell, Jr.

Whereas I Archabald Campbell Sr. [?] have this day for the love and affection I entertain for my son Archabald Campbell, Jr., and for the further consideration of his providing for me & my wife Rebecca Campbell a home and good comfortable food clothes & lodging and the taking good care of us in sickness or in health during our natural life and at my death & wife's death the [to be?] \*\*\* \*\*\* I do hereby give transfer and convey to him my tract of land in the State of Tennessee Wilson County containing by estimation one hundred acres of land by [being?] the same more or less which is bounded on the east by E. G. Campbell & J. S. Wommack [?] on the south by Mary Hel [Helt?] & others, on the west by W. Paul, & on the north by E. G. Campbell to have in whole [& hold?] to him the said Archabald Campbell Jr. & his heirs & assigns forever I do commit & *** myself to *** and *** the *** to the said Archabald Campbell his heirs and assigns against the lawful claims of all persons whatever. This conveyance is however made upon the above conditions that is if the said Archabald Campbell shall well & faithfully furnish us so long as we shall live with a comfortable house, good healthy food, comfortable clothing & all other *** *** for our comfort in *** and in sickness & at my wife's death a decent burial then & in that case the above tract of land is to be his & his heirs and assigns forever, but if he shall fail or refuse to provide for us according to the above then & in that case this conveyance shall be void & of no effect either in law or equity but so long as he provides for us as above the use and *** of the above land is his for him to live on & cultivate & use as his own but not to convey it at any time during the life of either of us in witness of which I have hereunto set my name and seal this 13 day of Feby 1854

**Item 5: 1856 August 5 Abstract of Will of Edward Gaither**

Daugher; Mildred Raines. Grandsons: Daniel G. Travis; Amos F. Gaither. Other property divided between Silas Gaither; Arther Gaither; Wilson Gaither; Mahala Tenpenny; Mary Ann Campbell; Mary Jane Tenpenny; Eliza Jane Sauls; heirs of Anna Campbell. Land set aside for family cemetery. Executors: Amos Gaither and Arthur Gaither.

Witnesses: Swenfild Smith; John H. Smith. Will signed 5 Aug. 1856, proved 11 Dec. 1856.

**Item 6: 1866 October 5 Abstract of the Will of Archibald Campbell (the Younger, Sr.)**

Son: Thomas Campbell. "My legitimate children excepted the above named one I will nothing." No executor named. Witnesses: Amos Gaither, Thomas Vance.

Source: p. 217 of original will book; in Gladys Carlson, ed., *Abstract of Cannon County, Tennessee Will Book Volume A (1836-1895) Based on the WPA Transcript* (n.d., Signal Mountain, Tennessee: Mountain Press), p. 13.

**Item 7: 1868 October 6 Guardianship Bond on the part of Thomas Campbell et al.**

State of Tennessee, Cannon County

Know all men by these presents that we, Thomas Campbell, Thomas Vance, and William Ready, all of Cannon County in the state aforesaid, are held and firmly bound unto the State of Tennessee in the sum of five hundred dollars to be paid to the said state as aforesaid in trust for the benefit of the children hereafter named committed to the tuition of the said Thomas Campbell, to which payment well and truly to be made we bind ourselves and each of us, each and every one of our homes, executors and administrators, jointly and jointly and severally, firmly by these presents, sealed with our seals and dated this 6th day of October 1868 – The condition of the above obligation is such that whereas the above bounden Thomas Campbell is constituted and appointed guardian to Matilda Morgan, Recia E. Morgan, James A. Morgan, Robert A. Morgan, Rebecca Morgan, Lydia J. Hayes & Manerva E. Hayes, minor heirs at law of Allen Morgan, deceased. Now if the said Thomas Campbell shall faithfully execute his guardianship by securing and improving all the estate of the said minors that shall come into his possession for the benefit of the minors, until they shall arrive at full age or be sooner thereto required and then render a plain and true account of his guardianship on oath before the the justices of of our said court, and deliver up, pay to, or possess the said minors of all such estate or estates as they ought to be possessed of, or to such other persons as shall be lawfully empowered or authorized to receive the same and the profits arising therefrom, then this obligation shall be void, otherwise to be and remain in full force and virtue.

Thomas Campbell {seal}
William Ready {seal}
Thomas Vance {seal}

Acknowledged and approved in open court Oct. 6th 1868

    J. A. Gooding, [***]

Registered Oct. the 7th 1868 Josephus Finly, Clerk

Source: Cannon County, Tennessee, Court Records, 1854-1872, film #12, page 462.

## Item 8: 1886 Will of Thomas Campbell

Thomas Campbell   } Cannon County, Tennessee Last Will & Testament } March 4th, 1886

I hereby convey unto my Sons John W. Campbell and Amos D. Campbell all of the Lands that I possess with the Exception of the apple orchard. Said lands to be valued and the proceeds to be Equally divided amongst my Bodily heirs Consisting of Mary Dobbs, Haly Vance, John W. Campbell, and Amos D. Campbell. The Orchard I wish to be Sold to the highest bidder among the heirs and the proceeds to go to that one Distributor I have. So far as it will go I want all the Remainder for my wife's benefit So long as She lives, but of the heirs will Support her with all the necessaries and comforts they Can take the Land and Make what they Can on it.

| | |
|---|---|
| Witnesses | |
| R.F. Tatum | his |
| R.R. Gaither | Thomas [x] Campbell |
| | mark |

# INDEX

Women are listed by maiden names

Alexander, Archibald ............................................................ 18-19, 23
"Allen" as middle name ........................................................ 58, 63, 88
American Revolution ............................................................ 31, 47, 48
Amey (slave of William Campbell) ..................................... 33, 35, 112
Argyll, including earls and dukes of Argyll ............... xi, 5, 10-12, 22
Armstrong, Clinton (b. 1860) ............................................................ 97
Armstrong, John Greer (b. 1838) ...................................................... 97
Armstrong, Mary Clista (b. 1861) ..................................................... 97
Armstrong, Pernetia ................................... see Witherspoon, Pernetia
Armstrong, Sam (b. 1860) .................................................................. 97
Armstrong, Thomas Knox (b. 1858) ................................................. 97
Augusta County, Virginia ..................................... 2, 17-18, 27, 31, 109
Ballew (Balliew, Bilyew) family ......................................................... 8
Baptist churches ........................................................................... 60, 68
Barrett, Matthew Reid ...................................................................... 107
Beaumont High School, Beaumont, Texas ....................................... 80
Beaumont, Texas ....................................................................... 1, 73-88
Belt, Nancy ................................................................................... 52, 96
Beverley Manor, Virginia .................................................................. 18
Big Lick, Virginia ............................................................ see Great Lick
Blalock, Kathryn Ann ...................................................................... 104
Boardman, Stephen ....................................................................... 9-10
Borden Tract, Virginia ....................................................................... 18
Botetourt County, Virginia .................................... 1, 2, 31-39, 111-115
Braxton, Tennessee ....................................................... 66-67, 68, 69, 77
Buna, Texas ........................................................................................ 79
Cammack, Adam Cecil (b. 1983) .................................................... 109
Cammack, Alexander James (b. 1992) ........................................... 109
Cammack, Autie Lucretia (b. 1926) ................................................ 105
Cammack, Carolyn Sue (b. 1963) ................................... 85-86, 87, 109
Cammack, Elizabeth Ann "Beth" (b. 1953) ............................. 85, 108
Cammack, James Elam "Jim" (b. 1961) .................................... 85, 109
Cammack, Lester Eugene (Sr., b. 1930) .................................... 85, 107
Cammack, Lester Eugene "Gene", Jr. (b. 1955) ....................... 85, 108
Cammack, Marilyn Marie (b. 1958) .......................................... 85, 109

Cammack, Matthew Eugene (b. 1979) .............................................. 109
Campbell DNA ................................................................................. 7-9
Campbell family or clan in Scotland ................................ xi, 1-2, 9-13
Campbell, Ada Inez (b. 1884) ........................................................ 100
Campbell, Ada Lois (b. 1917) ........................................................ 102
Campbell, Albert L. (b. 1870) ............................................ 60, 62, 100
Campbell, Alexander (b. 1788, founder of Churches of Christ) .... 68
Campbell, Alexander (b. 1919) ...................................................... 102
Campbell, Allan Gene (b. 1980) ..................................................... 106
Campbell, Allison (b. 1987) ........................................................... 107
Campbell, Alphenia (b. 1825) .......................................................... 95
Campbell, Amos (b. ca. 1815) .................................................... 50, 96
Campbell, Amos Dison (b. 1847) ...................................... 56, 58, 61, 99
Campbell, Archibald (father of Malcolm Campbell) ................. 21, 23
Campbell, Archibald "the Elder" (b. 1743) ...... 25, 31, 34, 93, 111-112
Campbell, Archibald "the Younger" (and Sr., b. ca. 1770) ...... 1-2, 3,
        30, 36, 38-39, 43-47, 49-54, 57, 636, 94, 96, 113, 116, 117
Campbell, Archibald Jr. (b. ca. 1815) ................. 50, 52, 53, 96, 115-116
Campbell, Billy Marion (b. 1936) ................................................... 103
Campbell, Buson (b. 1848) ...................................................... 56, 100
Campbell, Carl (b. ca. 1916) ........................................................... 103
Campbell, Carnell Tracy (b. 1904) .................................................. 101
Campbell, Chapman (b. 1829) .......................................................... 95
Campbell, Cheryl Lynn (b. 1978) ................................................... 106
Campbell, Chester (b. 1898) ........................................................... 101
Campbell, Clack R. (b. 1809) ............................................................ 94
Campbell, Coland Edward (b. 1910) .............................................. 102
Campbell, Colin, "Colin the Great" (d. ca. 1296) ............................ 10
Campbell, Colin, First Earl of Argyll (d. 1492-1493) ....................... 10
Campbell, Edward Dison (b. 1882) ......................................... 60, 101
Campbell, Edward Gaston (b. ca. 1806) .................................... 50, 96
Campbell, Elam Allen (b. 1898) ....................... 3, 68, 75, 76, 77-88, 104
Campbell, Elam Lawrence (b. 1991) .............................................. 107
Campbell, Elizabeth (b. 1747) ...................................... 25, 31, 33, 93, 111
Campbell, Elizabeth (b. ca. 1913) ................................................... 102
Campbell, Elizabeth Marie (b. 1986) .............................................. 106
Campbell, Everett Arden (b. 1924) ............. v, 5, 83-84, 84-85, 88, 104
Campbell, Gene Allen (b. 1926) .............................. 5, 83-84, 85, 105
Campbell, George Lee (b. 1873) ....................................................... 99

Campbell, Glen Ed (b. 1961) ..................................................... 85, 107
Campbell, Hiram Kirk (b. 1933) ..................................................... 103
Campbell, Ila Okla (b. 1908) ..................................................... 102
Campbell, James (possible brother of Malcolm Campbell) ........... 23
Campbell, James (b. ca. 1783) ...................... 31, 36, 38-39, 95, 113, 114
Campbell, James Allen (b. 1872) ........................... 3, 60, 62-72, 77, 103
Campbell, James Edward (b. 1880) ............................................... 100
Campbell, James M. (b. 1905) ....................................................... 102
Campbell, James Thomas "Jimmie" (b. 1902) .............. 68, 75, 76, 103
Campbell, James Thomas, Jr. (b. 1932) ......................................... 103
Campbell, Jane "Jean" (b. 1754) ..................... 25, 93, 111, 112
Campbell, Jesse Dison (b. 1875) ...................................................... 99
Campbell, John (possible brother of Malcolm Campbell) ............. 23
Campbell, John (b. ca. 1777) ........................... 30, 36, 37, 38-39, 94, 112
Campbell, John Hubert (b. 1938) ................................................... 104
Campbell, John "Johnny" (b. 1904) ............. 68, 75, 76, 80-81, 86, 101
Campbell, John Robert (b. 1870) ..................................................... 99
Campbell, John Watson (b. 1845) ..................... 3, 5, 6, 58, 59-62,
 66, 73, 90, 100, 119
Campbell, John William (b. 1902) ................................................. 101
Campbell, Kelly Ann (b. 1975) ................................................. 87, 104
Campbell, King Allen (b. 1947) .................................................. 84-85
Campbell, Leona (b. 1925) ............................................................. 102
Campbell, Lloyd ............................................................................. 1, 5
Campbell, Lorelle (b. 1915) ............................................................ 102
Campbell, Lou Ann (b. 1878) .......................................................... 99
Campbell, Lydia Anne (b. 1986) .................................................... 106
Campbell, Lydia J. "Liddy" (b. 1880) ....................................... 60, 101
Campbell, Madelyn Paige (b. 2008) ......................................... 88, 106
Campbell, Maggie Marie (b. 1930) .................... 83, 85-86, 87, 106
Campbell, Mahala "Mahaly" "Haly" (b. 1840) .................. 56, 97, 119
Campbell, Malcolm (b. ca. 1715).................................. 3, 20-29, 93, 111
Campbell, Margaret Tamzey (b. 1817) ............................................ 94
Campbell, Mark Elam (b. 1956) ................................................85, 106
Campbell, Martha Ann (b. 1820) .................................................... 95
Campbell, Mary (b. 1749) .................................................. 25, 93, 111
Campbell, Mary Ann (b. 1842) .............................................. 56, 98, 119
Campbell, Mary Ann (b. 1875) ................................................. 60, 101
Campbell, Matilda (b. 1814) ............................................................ 94

Campbell, Morgan Thomas (b. 1887) ................................. 60, 62, 102
Campbell, Nettie A. (b. 1885) ................................................. 60, 102
Campbell, Omer (b. 1897) .............................................................. 101
Campbell, Polly (b. ca. 1786) ........................... 31, 34, 36, 38, 95, 114
Campbell, Rebecca (b. 1751) ............................................ 25, 91, 109
Campbell, Rhoda "Rhody" (b. ca. 1784) ........... 31, 34, 36, 38, 95, 114
Campbell, Robert (b. 1804) ............................................................. 94
Campbell, Rosannah (b. 1868) ................................................ 60, 100
Campbell, Sally Laverne (b. 1940) ................................................ 104
Campbell, Seaton (b. 1823) ............................................................ 95
Campbell, Sephythia Isabell (b. 1882) ........................................... 100
Campbell, Serena Callie (b. 1877) ........................................... 60, 101
Campbell, Stephanie Alexandra (b. 1985) .................................... 105
Campbell, Susanna (b. 1808) .......................................................... 94
Campbell, Ted Allen (b. 1953) ................................................. 85, 105
Campbell, Thomas (b. 1763, founder of Churches of Christ) ........ 68
Campbell, Thomas (b. ca. 1773) .................. 30, 34, 36, 38-39, 111, 113
Campbell, Thomas (b. ca. 1807) ....................... 3, 50, 54-58, 59, 63
                                                                          88, 97, 117-119
Campbell, Thomas Allen (b. 1872) ................................................. 99
Campbell, Walter Erwin (b. 1912) ................................................. 102
Campbell, Warren Gene (b. 1948) ............................................ 85, 105
Campbell, Wesley (b. 1992) ........................................................... 107
Campbell, WIlliam (possible brother of Malcolm Campbell) ........ 23
Campbell, William (b. ca. 1750, "the Elder") ..................... 3, 4, 25, 28
                                                                          29-37, 93, 94, 111, 113-115
Campbell, William (b. ca. 1781, "Jr.") .............. 31, 36, 38-39, 113, 114
Campbell, General William of Kings Mountain ............................ 31
Cannon County, Tennessee ........................... 1, 2, 55-72, 74, 77, 87
Churches of Christ ........................................................ 68-69, 76, 81
Civil War .................................................................... 53-54, 57, 60
Cropper, Hiram (b. 1822) ............................................................... 95
Cropper, James ........................................................................ 46, 95
Cropper, Lovinda (b. 1802) ............................................................ 95
Curry, John ..................................................................................... 43
Curry, Mary .................................................................................... 43
Dabney, Susannah ........................... 30, 33, 34, 37, 46, 94, 114-115
Daniel (slave of William Campbell) ...................................... 33, 35, 113
Davenport, Laurena ....................................................................... 96

Dibrell, Tennessee .................................................................. 62
Dingo (slave of William Campbell) ..................... 33, 35, 114
Dixon, Sharon Sue (b. 1957) .............................................. 108
Dobbs, Ann S. (b. 1867) ....................................................... 98
Dobbs, Colista Angeline (b. 1874) ..................................... 98
Dobbs, James "Jim" (b. 1871) ............................................. 98
Dobbs, Jesse Howell (b. 1886) ............................................ 99
Dobbs, John Pittard (b. 1837) ............................................. 98
Dobbs, John P. (b. 1878) ...................................................... 98
Dobbs, Pernisia (b. 1879) .................................................... 98
Dobbs, Terah Jane (b. 1881) ................................................ 99
Dobbs, Thomas E. (b. 1869) ................................................ 98
Dyson, Mary ......................................................................... 55
"Elam" (name) ...................................................................... 77
Esslinger, Kelly (b. 1977) ................................................... 105
Esslinger, Pat .................................................... see Sandusky
Evans, Nathaniel ........................................................ 91, 112
Fick, Dale Marie (b. 1954) ................................................. 105
Forest Lawn Cemetery, Beaumont, Texas ................... 87-88
Forman, Angela Anderson ............................................... 105
Foss, Richard R., II ............................................................ 106
French and Indian War .............................................. 21, 26-27
Fuller, Virginia Cothran ................................................... 103
Gaither, Anna "Annie" (b. 1822) ........... 52, 55, 56-57, 97, 117
Gaither, Edward .................................................... 55, 57, 117
Gaither, Mary Ann ........................... 52, 53, 55, 57, 96, 117
Gaither, R. F. ......................................................................... 58
Gaither, Rachel (b. 1718) ............................................... 47, 55
Great Lick, Virginia .................... see also Roanoke; 18, 20-39
Grosso, David Allen (b. 2009) .................................... 88, 106
Grosso, David Michael (b. 1977) ..................................... 106
Hand, Stephanie Sue (b. 1950) ......................................... 105
Hardin County, Texas ........................................................ 80
Hayes, Rachel C. (b. 1832) .................................................. 65
Hipps, Elizabeth Ann "Betsy" (b. 1981) .......................... 108
Holland, Ambrose ......................................................... 46, 93
Houston surname ............................................... see Huston
Houston, Sam ............................................................... 19, 24
Hugus, Mary Louise "Lucy" (b. 1919) ............. 84-85, 88, 104

Huston, Isabella ..................................................... 21, 23-26, 28-29, 93
Ireland ................................................................. 13-14, 20, 22, 91
Islay (island of Scotland) ................................................... 22
Jackson, President Andrew ................................................ 41
Jacob, Jeremiah (b. 1712) ......................................... 47, 48, 55
Jacob, Rebecca ................................................................. 48
Jacobs, Edward G. ............................................... 45, 47-50, 51
Jacobs, Rebecca ........................... 46-47, 48, 49, 50, 52-53, 96, 115-116
Jefferson County, Texas .................................................... 2-3
Jura (island of Scotland) ................................................... 22
Kintyre Peninsula and the Mull of Kintyre ........................... 13
Lawrence County, Tennessee ............................................ 62
Locke's Creek, Cannon County, Tennessee ............. 55-56, 59-60
Lyle, Daniel ................................................................. 18-19, 23
Lyons, Bradley (b. 2006) ................................................ 88, 107
Lyons, Rachel ..................................................................... 107
McBroom Family Cemetery, Cannon County, Tennessee ........ 66, 71
McBroom, Henry D. ............................................................ 65
McBroom, James (b. 1827) .................................................... 65
McBroom, Nancy Elizabeth (b. 1852) ............................. 65, 67-68
McCollum, Nancy Orchid (b. 1956) ...................................... 109
McDonald, Edward ....................................................... 25-26, 29-30
McDonald, Elizabeth (b. 1753) ...................... 28, 29-30, 32-33, 94
McDonald, Rebecca ............................................................ 29
McGowan, Toni Ann (b. 1958) .......................................... 106
Magnolia Cemetery, Beaumont, Texas ......................... 76, 88
Maryland ......................................................................... 47-48
Maury County, Tennessee ................................................ 62
Maxwell, Arsenath ............................................................ 96
Methodist churches ............................................................ 81
Miller, Marion Nell (b. 1957) ............................................ 106
Mood, Jeannie Shannon (b. 1978) .................................... 106
Morgan, Allen ........................................................ 58, 59, 63, 88, 118
Morgan, Serecia "Recia" "Reacy" (b. 1845) ............... 59-62, 100, 118
Morgan, Serena (b. 1846) ........................................... 59, 60, 99
Moss, Elizabeth (b. 1880) ................................................. 101
Murrell, Britney Danyell (b. 2004) ................................ 88, 108
Murrell, Peyton Cooper (b. 2009) .................................. 88, 108
Murrell, Randall Dewayne ............................................... 108

Myers, Gary Christopher (b. 1986) .................................................. 109
Myers, Gary Wayne (b. 1984) ............................................................ 109
Myers, Jaime Marie (b. 1982) ............................................................ 109
Nashville, Tennessee ................................................................... 41, 71
Nederland, Texas ............................................................... 69-70, 73, 77
North Carolina ....................................................... 46-47, 48-49, 55, 65
Pegg (slave of Archibald Campbell the elder) .............................. 112
Pennsylvania ............................................................................. 22-23, 26
Philadelphia, Pennsylvania ................................................... 20, 21, 22
Plumley, Jason (b. 1981) .................................................................... 107
Presbyterian churches ........................................... 11-12, 14-15, 34, 60
Readyville Mill, Readyville, Tennessee ..................................... 59, 86
Reed, Elvie Hatten (b. 1879) ............................................................. 100
Revolutionary War ....................................... see American Revolution
Rieck, Anita (b. 1959) ........................................................................ 107
Roanoke, Virginia ................................ see also Great Lick; 18, 20, 21,
23, 27, 32-33, 37, 38-39
Robert the Bruce (Robert I, King of Scots) ....................................... 10
Rosedale Community, Jefferson County, Texas ....... 79-80, 81, 82, 86
Round Lick, Tennessee ...................... see also Watertown; 42, 43, 54
Sanders, Martha Blanche ................................................................. 104
Sandusky, Patricia Jean "Pat" (b. 1949) .......................................... 105
Sauls, Sally Ann ................................................................................ 105
Scotch-Irish ...................................................................... see Scots-Irish
Scotland ....................................................................... xi, 1-2, 7-15, 91
Scots Gaelic language .................................................................. 11-12
Scots-Irish .................................................................................. 1, 14-15
Shenandoah Valley, Virginia ............................................. 15, 17-18, 21
Simpson, Archibald ........................... 31, 33-34, 39, 43, 44, 45, 91, 112
Simpson, John ............................................................... 31, 33, 93, 112
Simpson, William ..................................................... 25, 31, 33, 93, 112
Slaves, slavery ..................................................... 4, 28, 33, 34, 35-36
Smith' Fork, Tennessee .......................... see also Statesville; 42, 54-55
South Park High School, Beaumont, Texas ................................ 76, 78
Spell, Annie Eliza ................................................................................ 79
Spindletop Oil Field ..................................................... 1, 73, 74-75, 78
Spugs, Myrtle Ellen ........................................................................... 103
Statesville, Tennessee ......................... see also Smith's Fork; 42-54-55
Stroud, Hiram ............................................................................... 69, 74

Sullivan, Herman .................................................................................. 69, 74
Sullivan, James T. ................................................................................ 65, 72
Sullivan, Lillie Ann (b. 1784) ................... 65, 66, 68, 72, 73-77, 89, 103
Sullivan, Margaret "Maggie" ............................................................ 69, 74
Sullivan, Raymond ...................................................................................... 74
Sullivan, Wiley ............................................................................................. 74
Summers, Mary ........................................................................................... 48
Summers, William ...................................................................................... 48
Taylor, Stephen A. ........................................................................... 20 (note)
Tennessee ................................................................................................ 41-73
Tenpenny Cave, Cannon County, Tennessee ............................. 61, 77
Tenpenny, Frances Parilee ................................................................. 60-61
Texas ............................................................................................ 69-70, 73-88
Thurston, John .......................................................................................... 101
Thurston, J. Lawrence ............................................................................ 101
Timber Ridge, Virginia .................................................................. 18-19, 23
Ulster ...................................................................................................... 13-14
Ulster Scots ........................................................................ 1, 13-14, 20-21
Vaught, Anna J. ........................................................................................... 96
Vaught, Esther L. ........................................................................................ 96
Virginia ................................................................................................. 15, 17-39
Walker, Dr. Thomas .............................................................................. 24-25
Warren County, Tennessee ..................................................................... 62
Watertown, Tennessee .................................. see also Round Lick; 42
"Western Country" .............................................................................. 35-39
Wilbanks, Coby Lee (b. 1981) ............................................................... 108
Wilbanks, Gerald Charles "Gerry" (b. 1953) ................................... 108
Wilbanks, Luke Patrick (b. 1982) ........................................................ 108
Wilbanks, Peter Allen (b. 2008) .................................................... 88, 108
Wilbanks, Susan Lyn (b. 1978) ............................................................. 108
Williams, Edward King ........................................................................... 79
Williams, Esther ......................................................................................... 96
Williams, Ola Lee "Jack" (or "Jackie," b. 1906) ............ 80-81, 86, 103
Williams, Stephen (b. 1760) ................................................................... 79
Williams, Verda Odessa (b. 1900) ........... 79-80, 82-83, 86, 87, 88, 104
Wilson County, Tennessee ........................................ 2, 41-55, 113-114
Winters, Elisha ................................................................................... 45-46, 95
Witherspoon, Pernecia "Pernetia" ............................................... 56, 100
Woodbury, Tennessee ........................................................................ 63, 67

129
Woodbury College .................................................................................. 63
World War I ........................................................................................... 79
World War II ..................................................................................... 83-84

www.ingramcontent.com/pod-product-compliance
Lightning Source LLC
Chambersburg PA
CBHW041622220426
43662CB00001B/22